Ships in Bottles

Revised and Expanded 2nd Edition

by Guy DeMarco

Schiffer Publishing Ltd

4880 Lower Valley Road, Atglen, PA 19310 USA

Acknowledgement

I again want to thank my son Guy for the wonderful drawings he produced for the first edition in 1985. They have been included in this revision as they originally appeared.

Designed by Bonnie M. Hensley
Type set in Seagull Hv BT/Humanast 521 BT

ISBN: 0-7643-0999-4
Printed in China

Published by Schiffer Publishing Ltd.
4880 Lower Valley Road
Atglen, PA 19310
Phone: (610) 593-1777; Fax: (610) 593-2002
E-mail: Schifferbk@aol.com
Please visit our web site catalog at **www.schifferbooks.com**

In Europe, Schiffer books are distributed by Bushwood Books
6 Marksbury Avenue Kew Gardens
Surrey TW9 4JF England
Phone: 44 (0)208-392-8585; Fax: 44 (0)208-392-9876
E-mail: Bushwd@aol.com
Free postage in the UK. Europe: air mail at cost.

This book may be purchased from the publisher.
Include $3.95 for shipping. Please try your bookstore first.
We are interested in hearing from authors with book ideas on related subjects.
You may write for a free printed catalog.

Contents

Preface

In a world where most hobbies require a strong commitment in dollars or time to complete a project, this romanticized art form is an oasis. It is in this fanciful miniature world with no large outlays of time, space, or money that we can escape the mundane and the pressures of the work-place to another time and place. This is indeed an ancient craft, with many museums proudly displaying antique attempts along with contemporary ones. Those ancient ones, built by sailors with little else then a jack knife and scraps of wood are most appealing to me. These men were the craftsmen, the dreamers, the artisans. At best we can mimic their art, with our steadier platforms, better tools and lighting, and supplies as needed only a short drive away.

When I first wrote this treatise I did so with younger hands, eyes and dreams. Now, almost sixteen years later, it seems that nothing has changed. Those things that were important to me then are still important now. Time, however has reached an urgency that I never knew existed back then.

My romance with the sea began at an early age. There were stories from my parents and grandparents of their Sicilian fishing village. My father helped and encouraged me with my early models. I can still remember them, him, and all the time he gave me.

As a "landlubber" my models were built from kits, plans, and pictures. In those days, ten cents bought a dry "clipper" model with a solid balsa block for the hull, printed balsa deck, and strip wood for the masts and spars. A raid on my mother's sewing basket rendered thread for the rigging. Toothpicks and dowels from medical swabs soon replaced the balsa masts. Armed with a ten-cent bottle of glue, a cork that always stuck and broke in the bottle, double-edged razor blades (with tape over one of the edges to protect my fingers), eyebrow tweezers, the family pair of scissors, pliers, and a box of pins, I was indeed ready to create, fabricating parts as needed.

There was little extra money back then to buy those expensive models for sale in the New York hobby shops, so almost every larger model I built was from scratch. I remember going to Polks on 32nd Street just to buy plans and some metal fittings that I didn't fabricate. I've been lucky in the fact that some of those early attempts have survived. They have been cleaned and repaired, calling back the years from their glass cases. I've been able to afford, build, and collect many of those sought-after models of my youth, with their well-turned brass fittings, scale cordage, and cast pieces that are like fine jewelers' work. This volume, and the art form it describes, takes me back full circle, to a ship craft where everything—including some of the tools—are scratch built.

With this in mind, let me take you on a journey, back a hundred years or so.

You are on the deck of a "windjammer" with the trade winds blowing steady as you come off watch. Your body, with its sea legs, is in tune with the pitch and roll of the deck. Cape Horn is a memory, and the coast of Brazil is off the port side. You're seated on the "fo'cstle" with the sun and wind at your back this balmy day. Within reach are your knife, pieces of wood, awl, needles and pins, along with bits of thread from the sail maker. Turning, you hold a bottle up to the sun, checking for impurities. Sighing, remembering how you emptied it that night in San Francisco, you begin...

Enjoy this craft of our forebearers.

Guy DeMarco

Chapter One
Bottle Choice and Sea Preparation

The container for the thing contained, always different, always a challenge.

As the famous actor once said "Ah, the stuff dreams are made of...." The container for the thing contained.

Round bottles are indeed the most common, with almost all wines and most cordials bottled in this way. However, if you have already leafed through this book, you will have noticed that I use many different shapes. In the beginning, choose one with a short neck and at least a ¾-inch mouth. Avoid the ones with fluted necks that bulge and constrict as these can be frustrating. At the moment of truth, the moment of insertion, you don't need this mechanical failure.

There have been times when I've browsed through liquor or package stores for bottles, catching wary glances from shopkeepers as I've turned bottles every which way, trying to examine shape, color, and neck size. Usually the best bottles have weird ingredients, but that's a matter of taste. Lately, I've been trying to build a collection based on the "Wines of America" trying to incorporate the label into the base. This is indeed a noble endeavor worthy of research including trips to vineyards and sundry wine tasting events. So far, the Pinot Noirs of Oregon... but that is another story. As a warning, do not try to empty the contents in the usual way, and then try to build and insert in the same evening. Steady hands and clear eyes are a necessity for this art form unless you're into surrealism. Picasso in a bottle is not what this is about.

After your choice is made, your first job is to clean the bottle. An overnight soaking in hot clear water with a little white vinegar will remove most of the labels and content residue. If the label gum is stubborn, a scouring pad will help. Let the bottle air dry neck down. I try to clean the streaks with a bit of paper towel attached to coat hanger wire. Always check for streaks. These are easy to clean while the bottle is empty.

I suggest that you measure the inside of the bottle with stiff paper templates. The purpose of this is obvious. I still have a ship on its trestle that was too tall for its intended container.

After the bottle is dry and clean, locate the casting seams. It's a good idea to mark these with a water soluble marker, since they will be your guide lines during the sea construction and ship insertion. Plan on having one of these lines as the center of your "sea" and the other to line up the masts. You never want the seam to mar your view, since the glass is always distorted in this area. Don't overlook the possibility of using a store-bought decanter. I have found some lovely ones and they're almost always blown bottles that are seamless.

If your choice of bottle was the round variety I would take the time to build a stand or cradle to hold it now. It's easier to maneuver the bottle while empty to get a snug and stable fit. I build the permanent one as well as a working cradle of scrap Styrofoam. The diagrams and photos are only meant to suggest. With the advent of art supply shops I now find decoupage plaques extremely useful. They exist in a variety of shapes and woods, and can easily be adapted to our particular use. A few years back I was trying to rush through one that I was going to give as a gift. Mr. Newton's second law also includes bottles rolling off tables.

There are several ways of manufacturing the sea. I have used all the types I describe. Each has its advantages and disadvantages. The sea itself could be calm as the ship is at anchor or whitecapped in a slight gale. I like the whitecaps and a ship's wake, as though it's sailing in the bottle, but again this is a matter of taste.

Carved Wooden Ocean

In this technique, the "sea" is fabricated from several wooden slats that will lie side by side in the bottle (see the next chapter for types and sources). I have used basswood in the past but hard balsa works just as well. Pick a width that can fit comfortably through the neck of the bottle. If your bottle choice is a complete round one, prepare now a sub-base of either clay, putty, or wood slats to accept the finished "sea" as a flat surface inside the bottle. It is best to use sea blanks for fit before the task of carving and/or molding. Holding this sea platform together with the aid of duct tape, you can place it face up on the work bench. Marking off the position of the "hull blank" you can begin to design the sea with bow wave, wake, whitecaps and even shark fins.

At this point you have two choices. The wood can either be carved to design, or it can be a base for sculpting the sea. If you choose the latter, balsa filler, plastic wood, and even automotive body filler can be used as the molding medium. The historic ones were carved, but why not take advantage of materials available? You can even use the clays described later on in conjunction with this platform method. Taking one's time, a spectactular result can be achieved.

Going on the asumption that you will either carve or mold the ocean, the next plateau is the finish. Water is wet, and wet is shiny. To belabor the obvious is indeed my intention. First, the finished ocean must be sealed so as not to appear porous. Two or three coats of a sanding sealer will suffice. Keep checking the parting lines so that they can still break free after each coat. A deep blue-green paint is the best to contrast with the white caps and wake. I have dry-brushed the tips of the waves just below the whitecaps to give the appearance of shallow water.

Use an off-white for the caps since pure whites tend to maginfy when viewed from a distance. Take your time and keep placing the hull blank in position for a visual check. To achieve the "wet" look one or two coats of gloss lacquer will suffice. There are several aerosols available in both hobby and paint stores that are acceptable. Let this "sea air" dry for a few days to release all of the gases, especially if you used a lacquer-based paint for color or sealing. The finished product inside a sealed bottle will eventually give up any trapped medium and cloud the glass. I'll repeat this warning several times in this tome: **never use a water-based adhesive to glue the hull to the sea.** It takes several hours to dry and cure this stuff and the clouding effect is a complete diasaster.

After the sea is finished it can be parted carefully to be placed in the bottle.

Air Hardening Clay

Most ceramic shops and art supply houses sell this under many brand names. It is widely used in both high school and college art classes as a molding medium for use without kiln drying. It dries to a porous wheat color. You will not have the advantage of being able to paint this "ocean" at your work bench, so it has to be painted inside the bottle.

Begin by inserting sausage-shaped pieces of clay. To avoid the mess of insertion I use bamboo food skewers to steady the clay through the neck. Since this clay is water-based, cleanup of the neck and sides may be time consuming, but it is possible with paper towels dampened with water or window cleaner. Using the improvised tools described in the next chapter mold the sea. Press in a hull blank to form the depression for the completed model. Before painting, let the "sea" dry for several days. Several brands will cloud the bottle during this process. Again, cleanup is required here.

Painting will present its own aquired skills, as the brushes themselves become somewhat of a balancing act. Use only acrylic paints, since laquer will definitely cloud while drying and will require a lacquer thinner for cleanup, which also clouds. To achieve the "wet" look of the ocean you can use any one of several water-based gloss finishes that are sold for decoupage or hobby use. A credible job can be done with diluted white glue allowed to dry for several days. Again, you can clean up the clouding with window cleaner at the end.

Plasticine

This is the "clay" of our childhood, evoking memories of rainy days in grammar school, blobs thrown at friends behind the teacher's back and caught under our finger nails, warnings from Mom never to use it in a carpeted room, and that oily smell that never left our senses.

I have found this the easiest to use with insertion techniques described before. Cleanup and clouding is minimal. With the advent of modern technology and chemistry, there are now many brands offered for sale in a virtual rainbow of colors. Some even air dry when left exposed. I have combined greens, blues, and black for the sea base and thin strips of white for wakes, bow waves and white caps. Point of fact, final molding can be done after the ship is inserted to simulate the effect of it actually sailing in the water. All of the models presented are sailing on clay seas.

I have used all three of these methods, even in combination. The colored clay as a molding technique with a wooden base, air hardening clay in conjunction with a carved ocean for emphasis. The best part of this craft is the experimentation. No two models are ever built, "sailed," or presented in the same way. Bottles are relatively easy to come by, so don't waste time or build up a frustration based on an irrevocable task. Mistakes can be discarded. Time, with this or any other hobby, cannot be your enemy.

The completed model should have a look of harmony with the ocean waves.

Chapter Two
Tools and Materials

Wherein the crafty mariner learned to improvise.

The natures of this hobby are twofold. First, it is compact. You are indeed able to store all of your materials in an art supply, tackle, or shoe box. That makes this hobby a portable one, with workspace almost anywhere in the house or on the road. Second, it exercises your ability to improvise. Many of the hand-built tools can embellished by you the modeler. I describe the ones that work for me, that I found by trial, error, and sometimes luck born of desperation, but nothing is truly set in concrete. Improvisation is expected here.

I have taken the liberty to rate the store bought tools from one to three. The (1) being an absolute necessity to the (3) being a luxury.

Modeling Tools

Scissors (1)
Necessary for cutting sails and thread. Some of the fine ones used for sewing work best for the fine and delicate cuts they make.

Craft or hobby knives (1)
Excellent because of the replaceable knife and chisel blades. One handle can be used for almost all carving needs, although the knife assortment chests are best in the long run. These can range from simple assortment to the truly exotic depending on your budget. I've had mine for almost forty years now with many blade replacements. Lately, with the advent of the "box cutter" and its breakaway blade to insure constant sharpness, a general replacement can be used. I use them sometimes, but their blade shape while always being sharp doesn't offer the variety of the replaceable ones.

Razor saw and mitre box (2)
Nothing finer for cutting hull blocks from wood stock. They are made to fit craft knife handles.

Pin vise and drill bits (1)
This is the small hand-twist drill used by jewelers and watchmakers. Again, hobby and craft stores carry these along with drill bit assortments. The numbers 70 through 80 are the best for our purposes. Keep several on hand as they tend to break easily if too much pressure is applied, and they do tend to dull quickly.

Small wire cutters (1)
Also called diagonal cutters. This tool became an absolute necessity to me while trimming rigging. I tend to use a CA glue for this and it dries the cordage to a "fine wire like" consistency. I found these invaluable for close in cutting on the completed model.

Tweezers (1)
I have several varieties with long and short barrels. The long dentist types are excellent in the final erection process. An added luxury for your tool box is a pair of tweezers used by stamp collectors. These will not crease the paper sails as they are attached to the masts.

Clamps (3)
Excellent for holding down deck planking while drying. There are nylon ones available now that resist most glue and will not mar a model with pressure lines.

Small pliers (1)
Invaluable for bending wire for the mast hinges.

Fine-edged ruler (1)
Necessary for transferring measurements and sail making.

Toothpicks (1)
What more needs to be said for these? Great for glue application, and in a pinch can be shaped and used for spars.

Lead pencils and fine markers (1)
For scoring seams on sails, flag making, and deck planking. Numbers 2 to 4 H work best. Mechanical pencils used in drafting have replaceable leads in very fine diameters. I use the .3m size in a 2H thickness.

Sail paper (1)
Almost any fine bond paper will do here. Again the hobby or craft store sells bond paper in a wide variety of colors for origami, decoupage, print or stationary making. The supply and variety is endless. Several of my friends through this hobby have had success with "silk span". This is a product used in the model airplane hobby. It comes in various thickness and is somewhat translucent. The thinner the better for our purposes.

French curve (3)
Used for creating the windblown effect in sails, as well as marking dead rise curve on the hull blocks.

Motor tool (3)

This is one of those luxuries that once used will never be discarded. They come in many different sizes and types. Some are variable speed, battery operated, and even with foot petal controls. The variety of bits is endless. I use this constantly to shape, smooth and polish hulls. This allows me the luxury of wood choice ranging from bass, cherry, oak, mahogany and maple. Many of these exotic woods show up in various sizes in most doll house supply stores. The motor tool allows for fine shaping without the wood splintering. As a word of caution here, it is advisable to use a face mask while sanding some of these hardwoods, as the dust is finer than most sawdust and can cause a problem. The ones painters use while finishing plaster walls are both inexpensive and disposable.

Brushes (1)

Several sizes are necessary with the #1 and 2 being used for hull painting and spar staining, with the #00 and smaller being used for whitecaps on painted "seas". The handles can be extended with the use of dowels and duct tape. A trip to an art supply store lead to discovery of a series of brushes with the last inch near the bristles bent at 90 degrees. They must have had this hobby in mind when there were invented.

Files (2)

Flat, round, or jewelers' shapes for finishing hulls and spars.

Sandpaper (1)

An absolute must for final finishing, spar and mast turning. Hardware stores and most supermarkets carry standard assortment packages. The wet or dry is the best as the grits tend to be finer. Again the hobby specialty shops carry some of the finest grits I've seen to be used in most modeling hobbies. Don't overlook the use of emery boards available at drug stores as nail files.

Needles and pins (1)

Straight pins are a necessity for mast hinges and useful in fabricating parts and fasteners while parts are drying. On smaller models they can be used for booms and spars. If necessity is indeed the mother of invention a needle imbedded in a piece of wood or dowel and heated over the stove to a red hot tip can do a credible jog of boring a hole through a mast or spar. Staples are a good source of fine wire to be used for hinges and such.

Sea Tools

Knitting needles (1)

These can be bent into various shapes as needed for inserting the sea clay. The back end can be used to scoop out the clay cradle for the hull. While were on the topic I "liberated" several crochet needles from my wife. There special shaped tips are useful to free snagged rigging inside the bottle.

Wire hangers (1)

Always in constant supply in every closet (in fact, I'm convinced that these things breed and multiply in dark places). Absolutely invaluable in forming seas, inserting clay, holding knife blades for cutting and shaping, and holding paper toweling or cotton balls for cleaning the inside of bottles. They are easy to bend, shape and cut.

Rubber tubing (2)

A bit of this attached to a knitting needle or hanger wire is useful in texturing the clay seas.

Erecting Tools

I began with a half dozen or so 3/16-inch dowels, some thin wire (sewing thread is just as good) for binding, safety pins, and single-edged razor blades. From these I fashioned what I call my lances (see illustrations).

(a) Straight lance: For picking at snagged rigging, untangling lines, repositioning clay sea after ship is bottled. I use several of these made with safety pins, thick and thin wire, as well as straight pins for various tips.

(b) Curved lance: Same as above but with sundry curved tips.

(c) Bent lance: Again, same as above but with different shaped tips. I mention these three separately since in all cases the tips are pre-formed before use. The hardness of the tips is important. You do not want these tools reshaping themselves while in use.

Cutting lances: (see illustrations) These are fabricated from the dowels and razor blades. Shielding your eyes and with the aid of a pair of pliers break off several pieces of blade. Using a knife or saw blade cut the dowels in the following fashion. These are almost mandatory in removing excess cordage from inside the bottle. Keep extra bits of blades handy since the almost surgical sharpness is necessary. Blade parts can be glued to the lance with CA cement.

(f) Back cutting: The sharp part of the blade faces forward for cuts under the bowsprit

(g) Down cutting: The blade tip is 90 degrees from the lance. Used in cutting boom and gaff stays.

(h) Forward cutting: An alternative for bowsprit trim.

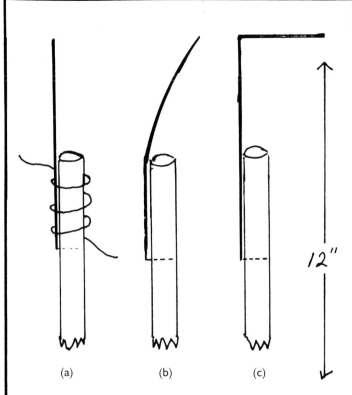

(a)   (b)   (c)

12"

With these lances, as well as several others of your design, the farthest recesses of any bottle can be reached. Imbed one end, lash, and glue to prevent swiveling.

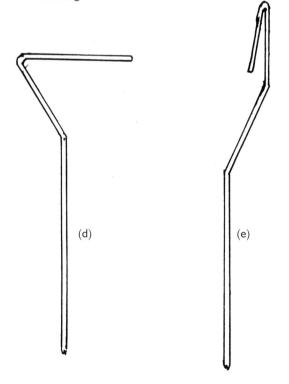

(d)   (e)

Wire form coat hangers can be built to any shape. The shape (d) is excellent for planting the model in the clay "seas" whereas (e) can be used for forming "waves". Experiment with design and shape for each different bottle.

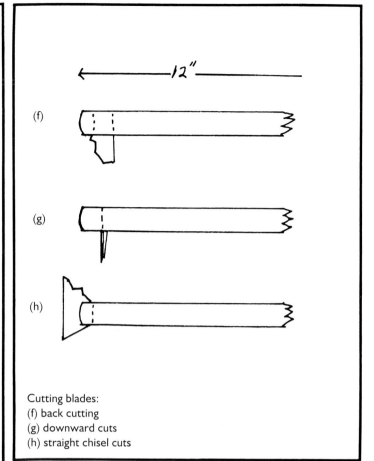

← —— 12" ——

(f)

(g)

(h)

Cutting blades:
(f) back cutting
(g) downward cuts
(h) straight chisel cuts

Materials

Wood stock

Many hobby and craft shops have entire sections devoted to doll house and model railroad construction as well as ships and planes. Varieties of woods range from soft balsa to the bass, cherry and oak mentioned earlier. In addition they come precut in a wide variety of strip sizes.

If you intend to stain rather than paint portions of your model bass is the best. However, it might be wise to investigate the darker woods if you choose a natural finish. Again, you will note from my finished models that I incorporated both.

Strip wood

a. 3/8 x 5/8 x 20 inches. The ideal size for carving hull blanks. This is available in the darker woods as well.

b. 1/16 square, 1/16 x 1/32, 1/64, etc. These are usually available packaged under scale strip wood for HO trains with sizes both in inches and millimeters. Useful for bulwarks, strakes, and rub rails. In a pinch, larger sizes can be sanded down, or heavy cardboard used in its place. Some of the prepackaged doll house wood is available in these small sizes in the darker woods as well.

c. 1/2 x 3/4-inch stock for the "erecting trestle" at the end of this chapter.

d. Scribed wood sheathing: Available in 1/16 x 3 x 20 inch bass with scribed surfaces. The scribing varies and again this is a matter of finding the right one. I have found the scribing as small as 1/64 inch and panel thickness to 1/32 inch. If not readily available a credible job can be done with a sharp knife blade to scribe a deck, or for that matter deck planks can be simulated with that mechanical drawing pencil.

Again, try to avoid balsa since it can never sand to a fine-edged finish and is much too soft for our mechanical needs.

Dowels

They're usually made of birch. 1/16 diameter for mast, spars, gaffs, and booms. The 3/16 to 1/4 are ideal for the lances. Again some of the specialty model supply houses dedicated to ship building are a source of supply. They even have dowels in the harder woods as well.

Metal Stock

Thin brass wire is available at most hobby supply outfits. This is useful for lance tips, mast hinges, simulation of cannons etc. I have found thin diameter aluminum tubing useful for my brush extensions and lance rods.

Adhesives

I can recommend three types here.

1. **CA adhesive:** Quick drying, will not decay, and will bond any surface texture and material to any other, **including fingertips.** Every hobby shop carries this product under several different brand names. However, if it spots the inside glass of the bottle it can be scraped off. I keep a bottle of nail polish remover and cotton swabs nearby when I'm using this for instant cleanup of my hands. Because of its penetrating capabilities I use this product to soak sections of masts and spars that require drilling. This changes the woods characteristics to an almost plastic like consistency that adds strength and the woods ability to split at the ends. The hinged base of all the masts are susceptible to split since the drilled hole is at best 1/8 inch above the end.

2. **Airplane glue**: Your basic cement in a tube. Its been around for as long as I can remember. It can still serve its purpose but it still tends to clump at the joint.

3. **Carpenter's or white craft glue:** This is the only glue type I recommend for sails to spars. CA and airplane glue change both texture and color of the sail material.

Paints and Stains

Hobby and art supply shops carry wide varieties of these in every color of the rainbow. I would suggest the use of acrylics whenever possible. You are doing close-in work, and breathing lacquer fumes is not healthy. Stains can either be brushed or rubbed to achieve that warm finish. Iodine, yes, iodine, was used as a cellulose indicator in biology labs for years in staining cells. It is perfect here as it will give both decking and masts a pale old wood finish.

Cordage

Shoemaker's thread, thread and cordage from the model supply houses, as well as some sewing threads are all applicable here. My favorite is fly tie line from the fresh water fishing supply counters. You will need two colors. Black or dark brown will be used for the standing rigging—in the real world of old ships this cordage was tarred to preserve it. Next, use light gray or natural for the running rigging.

Just a brief note: I used heavier cordage than normal on most of the photographed models so the rigging would stand out. In actual practice, the thinner the better. If you are using nylon rather than cotton, be careful as the CA adhesives tend to stiffen this a bit. Test out the glues on the threads that you ultimately use.

Embellishments

Over the years of model building I have a large scrap box of many parts from half-done, redone and never-started projects. I've used belaying pins from larger-scale models for cannons and capstans in models of this size. HO and N gauge bells intended for train models have become ships bells. Seed beads and hook eyes have found their use as well.

This entire chapter was devoted to materials and tools that were never available to those ancient mariners. If you have a mind to you could scrap all my suggestions and try to model as they did with a jack knife, scraps of wood and bamboo, oakum or pitch from the deck joints, a few scraps of thread, awl, and needles from their sewing kits. This would indeed be a modeling experience for all of us.

The Rigging or Erecting Trestle

I knew quite early in this hobby that my fingers were not small or nimble enough to steady the many parts of construction. This is more of an adaptation of my mechanical engineering/physics background then it is modeling. I used various forms of this over the years and in its final evolution I've come up with this. There are several factors that led to its design that I would like to share with you before you begin your journey into this miniature world.

1. It must be stationary as well as stable.
2. It must be light and portable enough to allow access to all parts of the model at any time.
3. That the model has the ability to be test-collapsed at any time (in case you haven't figured it out by now, my models are built outside the bottle and fitted in afterwards).
4. It must give you the ability to differentiate the strings.
5. It must have the ability to relieve the frontal pressure on the bowsprit, lest this piece collapse under the strain of the several cords passing through it.
6. It must be adaptable, since every model is different.
7. It must be quick to make, with the easiest of tools.
8. It should be reusable.

The trestle is built from basic pine wood or similar material. I used stop stock that is 1/2 x 3/4 inch from the local lumber yard. You could use strip basswood from the hobby supply places as well. The mainframe is 12 inches and the cross piece 6 inches, but these measurements are not absolutely critical. A simple lap joint three inches from one end as well as the center of the cross piece mount the smaller to the larger. Any glue will do at this joint.

Use brads or small-headed nails along the cross member. These serve as bits to secure the lines.

Several screw eyes are placed on the main member to force the lines that reeve through the bowsprit downward before they are secured to the brads. Keep several screw eyes handy to fairlead cordage away from the hull, spars and sails.

The actual hull is screwed with a thin wood screw at the back of the trestle. See the diagrams and photos in the following chapters to exemplify this.

As a sidebar to this construction I built more than one trestle. You may have several projects or ideas for ships at one time.

Rigging Trestle
1/2 Scale

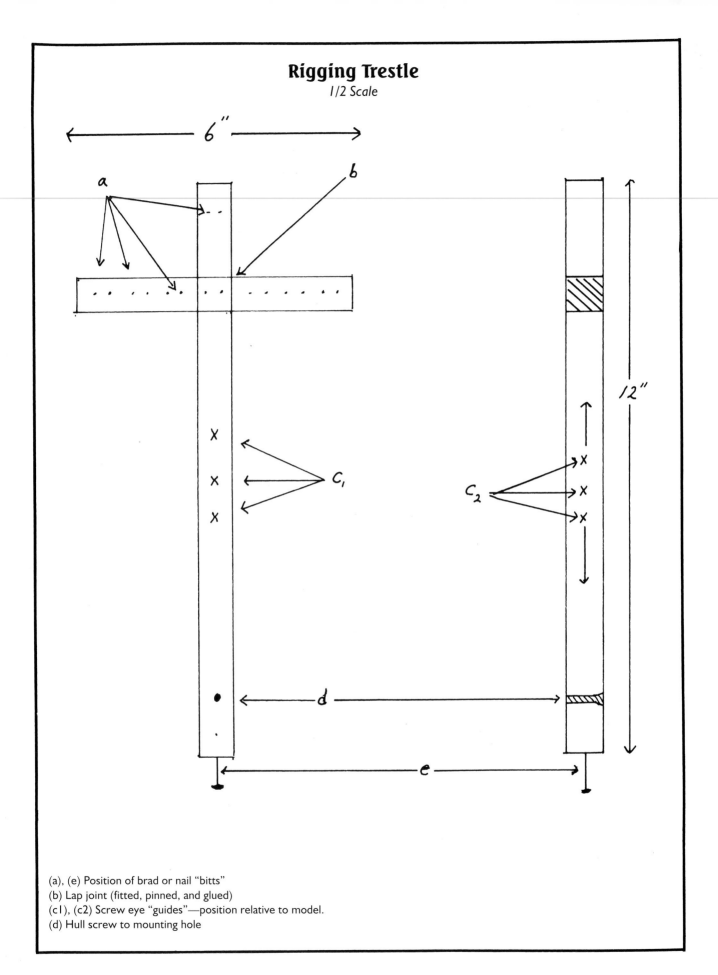

(a), (e) Position of brad or nail "bitts"
(b) Lap joint (fitted, pinned, and glued)
(c1), (c2) Screw eye "guides"—position relative to model.
(d) Hull screw to mounting hole

Chapter Three
Hulls, Masts, and Spars
The ancient art of woodcarving, shaping and assembling

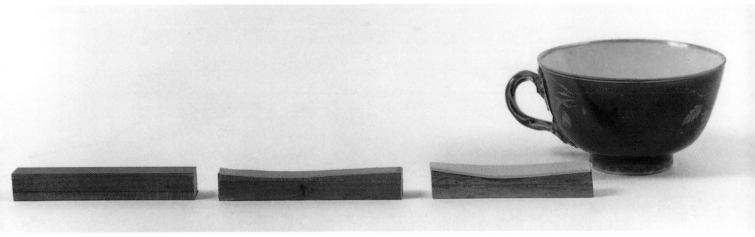

The first three stages of hull construction from port to starboard. Left to right: The hull blank, the hull with the dead rise carved in, the hull with deck planking strip in place. The teacup is shown for relative size.

As the Mad Hatter said to Alice, "You must begin at the beginning..." The hull blank is indeed our beginning. Use a close-grained block of wood smooth on at least two sides. Mark off the dead rise and carve the belly out first. Finish off with sandpaper. This is where the scribed deck will mount, so make sure it is smooth and without waves. Wood filler can do just so much. Next, mark, measure, and carve the hull blank from the deck view. At this point you will have what I will call the hull blank. Test fit in the bottle neck. If a sledge hammer is not necessary to make it fit, you're on your way. When you begin to shape the hull according the various plans in the following chapters, re-member that you are building a "waterline" model, so it should have a flat bottom. After the hull is rough-sanded, add the deck planking wood, holding in place until it dries with clamps or rubber bands. Trim the planking to con-form to the hull.

After this is dry add the bulwarks. In most cases I used 1/32 x 1/16-inch strip wood stock for these. Soak the wood to avoid splitting before gluing. After drying, finish with fine sand paper. Be careful, 1/32 wood does not allow much room for error. At this point measure off from the plan where the shrouds will enter the bulwark. Soak this area in CA glue for strength. It will fill the pores of the wood and still drill easily. It can still be painted over without chang-ing paint texture.

When I am not using natural woods I prefer to give the hull a coat or two of sanding sealer to fill the pores. Sand carefully after each coat has dried. Before the hull is painted, you might want to stain the deck using any of the methods in the last chapter. I still like the iodine. Any stain when rubbed off will fill the scribe lines, accentuating the deck planking. Now paint the hull with the appropriate color scheme.

After the hull is dried, mount to the rigging trestle. From now on, all work will be done to the mounted hull. You'll find it much easier to handle this way. If your particular model calls for cap rails, rub rails, and tran-som, it should be added now. If stripwood cannot be found in an appropriate thinness, then brown craft pa-per can be used cut into very fine strips. In the famous words of baseball philosopher Yogi Berra (changed ever so slightly), "half of this game is 90 percent improvisa-tion."

After adding all the deck furniture, remove from the trestle and test fit again through the bottle. Ideally it should fit in the lower half of the circular opening, leaving the up-per half free for masts, spars, and sails. If the hull is too high use rough sandpaper and sand wood off the bottom **NOW.** Keep test fitting before going any further, since this problem will not correct itself. You didn't come this far to put a ship in a pickle jar.

Stages in Hull Preparation

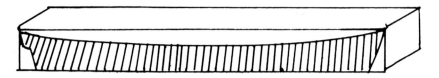

1. Profile is marked out from plan pattern. Use fine paper to trace plan.

2. Deck profile is traced and carved. Try to keep edges sharp.

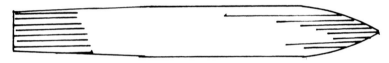

3. Deck planking is applied and cut to shape.

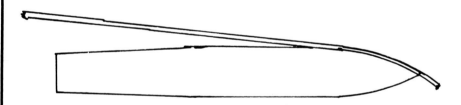

4. Bullwarks are formed by steaming or wetting wood stock. Apply a section at a time. Wait for drying before gluing the next. Trim and be careful sanding.

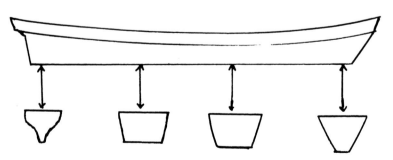

5. Form hull according to template sections. Test fit before finishing and painting.

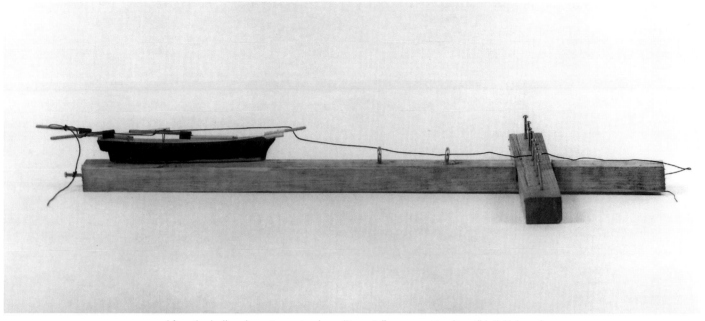

After the hull and masts are in place, "jury rig" one erecting line. (Hull *Alabama*)

Test-collapse, checking for bullwark clearance. At this point remove ship and test-collapse in bottle before checking for height as well as neck clearance. (*Alabama*)

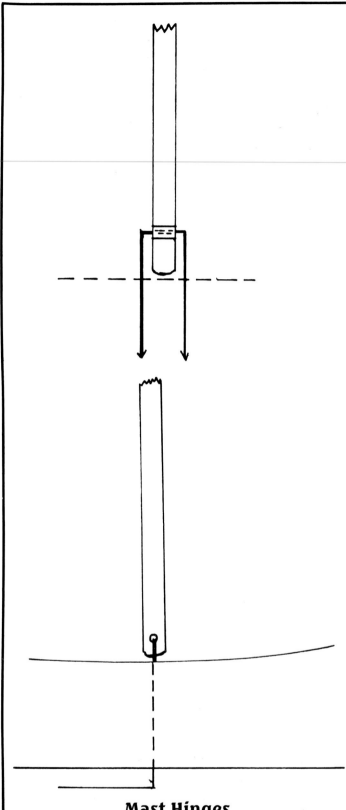

Mast Hinges

Before attempting to drill a hole this close to the edge of the dowel, soak end in crazy glue and let dry. This will prevent the mast from splitting or chipping. Form a staple shape from the brass wire, pin wire, or a safety pin. Mast should rotate freely at joint. For added strength, drill directly through the hull, and if the wire is long enough, let the excess be used as both an extra support for the mast as well as an anchor for the "sea clay".

After the hull is securely fastened to the trestle, make up the bowsprit. This spar should be tapered, however its best to drill all the necessary holes before tapering. Those emery boards are your best tool here, although sandpaper will work as well. This is the only secure spar on the ship. It should be glued securely and pinned down if possible. Again, soak this fully in CA cement to avoid splitting. The hole can be redrilled after this glue filler has dried thoroughly. After the bowsprit is secure with the correct rake, a cut water can be fashioned from your 1/16 x 3/16 stock. It should fit snug under the bowsprit. Paint to match the hull. The strakes or wales of the ship were designed as rub rails to protect the hull dockside. They can be fashioned with the thinnest of strip woods or use rigging thread stiffened in CA and painted a contrasting color. The wales should meet the cut water. Using a toothpick to apply the glue is a good idea for this assembly point.

The masts are your next logical step. Refer to the ships plans and measure to fit. Taper all top masts as you did the bowsprit.

Most of the models in the next chapters require a "made mast" of several pieces of dowel attached at a "doubling". If the plan calls for more than three shroud lines it is next to impossible to get through a small hole in a 1/16 inch dowel. If the masts are to be stained do that first after forming and tapering before you reinforce with CA glue. It is best that you drill through a point on the doubling. The heel of the mast is now drilled after a glue soaking and the mast hinges formed. (See diagram) This hinge is going to function more than once so make sure it freely rotates. After the masts are stepped, that is hinged to the hull, jury rig a single line and try and fit through the neck of the bottle. Get used to the test fitting idea several times in the early construction process.

Booms, gaffs, and spars will not have any holes drilled in them. Even though you may cut them from 1/16 dowel it is best to thin them out. I've tried stiff wire for some very small spars, but the wooden ones always appear to be better for me since I stain all my wooden parts. Take your time in thinning the dowels down, as their strength seems to be in the middle of their structure. At this stage of construction all your woodwork is done. If you follow the examples in the diagrams of the tying of the spars, they should swivel free since they must enter the bottle parallel to the masts and then swivel to their respective perpendicular status. Sails were "stitched" to the booms and gaffs as they were with the spars. The will have their own run through strings. I glue the strings before simulating the windings with natural cordage. Fly tie line is both thin and the right color.

At this stage of construction all your major woodwork is complete. Don't be afraid to "deep six" any part of the construction that doesn't measure up to your scrutiny. Others will never judge your work as harshly as you can, but you are the one it must satisfy.

Completely rigged *Victorine*, less sails.

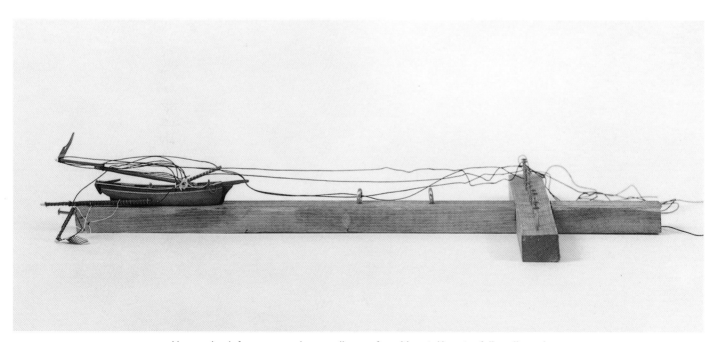

Always check for snags, and test-collapse often. Here is *Victorine* fully collapsed.

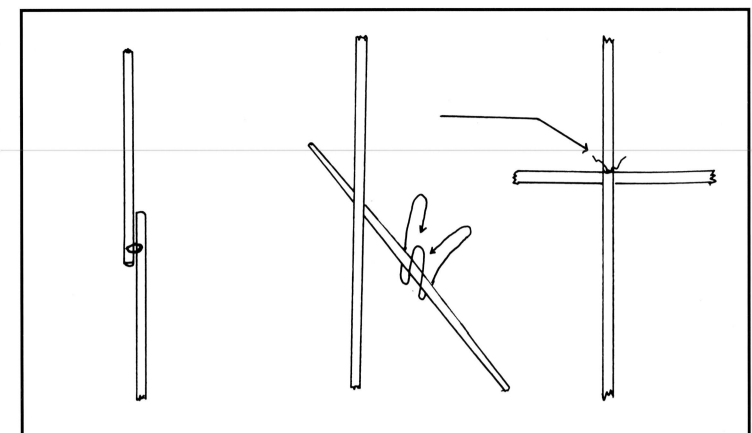

Drill hole for shrouds through mast joint for greater strength whenever possible.

Simple clove hitch glued only at yard front and mast knot will allow yard to be "cock-billed".

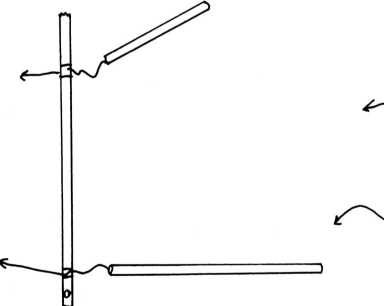

Run-through strings for gaff and boom allow greater flexibility when inserting ship. Lines can be run through "eyes" on the trestle side to keep them clear of shrouds, masts, and yards.

Most booms, gaffs, and clubs had sails "stitched" to them. These spars can be prepared by winding with the finest of threads and glued. If the thread is too obvious, tone it down with stain.

Chapter Four
Rigging and Sails

Tying of strings, splicing of cord, and hoisting of sails

The rig of a vessel has two major functions, to support the masts and spars, and to operate the sails. The former is called standing rigging, the latter running. Standing rigging was usually tarred to protect it against the elements, and is best represented by black or dark brown thread. The running rigging had to move through assorted blocks, tackles, fair leads and pulleys and therefore protection was not possible. Use an off-white or natural (tan) thread for this. In addition, our models have a third type, the rigging needed for raising the masts and sails. I have incorporated this as part of the standing rigging, hence black or dark brown. All of the plans in this book have separate diagrams for standing and running rigging, with the erecting lines clearly labeled. Follow these diagrams and this thing of ours will work.

Start with the shroud lines first. Drill appropriate holes through the bulwarks where they meet the deck. **All shroud line holes must be drilled behind the line of the mast, otherwise it will not collapse backward for insertion.** After the mast is stepped on the deck with its free swinging hinge, we'll begin to thread the shrouds using a length of cordage approximately twice the length needed. Begin by knotting one end; now here is a neat trick: soak about two inches of the other end in CA glue. Draw it taught and let it dry. Now that it's quite stiff use your sharpest blade and cut it on a 60 degree angle or so. *Voila!*—that's a French word meaning holy cow or something—you have a built-in needle. If after two or three passes this needle dulls, just trim a new point. Starting with the forward-most hole, begin to thread the shrouds from side to side, from the inside out and through the mast hole.

After all the lines are placed, check the rake of the mast and the pitch to both left and right (port and starboard). When satisfied with the pitch, a drop of glue at the mast hole and the bulwarks will make this permanent.

The next part of the project is the erecting and run through strings. I have tried to keep these down to an absolute minimum. On models with multiple masts I've tried to disguise these as fore stays and mainstays serving both purposes. After each string is rigged, touch the ends with a drop of CA and snip close when dry. These strings should be about 15 to 18 inches long since they must ultimately run through the bowsprit and outside the bottle in almost all cases. The mast tips where these cords end were usu-

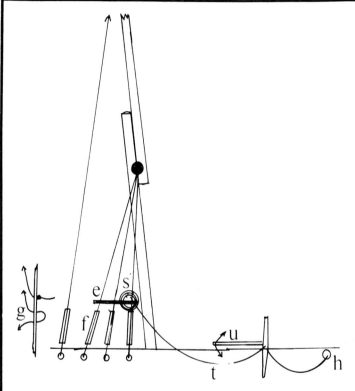

Standing Rigging

The shrouds are set by knotting the first one through its bulwark hole and gluing (g). They are now threaded through the bulwark and up through the mast to the other side. Draw tight before final glue is applied.

Heavy white or beige paint is applied at these sections to simulate deadeye assembly (f).

A thin piece of wood or pre-glued string is applied to simulate spreader.

The anchor assembly is made of pre-glued black string and wood for shank. It is lashed to the caprail with (t) the excess rope coiled to the shrouds (s). The anchor cable passes through a hawse hole in the bulwark. (See *Victorine*)

ally painted buff or black. This painting will draw attention away from the knots. After each string is threaded, test-collapse. Here is where the brads on the rigging trestle earn their keep. Each erecting string is in passes through the bowsprit, down to the hook eye and lashed around several of the brads. The photos clearly show this.

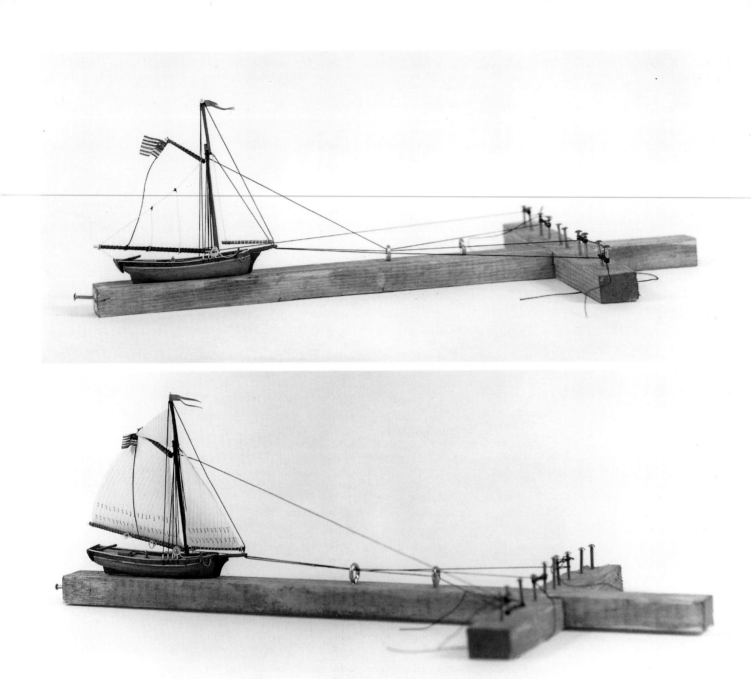

Here is our little *Victorine* with and without sails. Either way, she still has to fit through the neck.

All shrouds were tightened by a series of "dead eyes". These were compound pulleys of three strands. You can simulate this with some off-white paint applied to the ends of the shroud lines about 1/8 of an inch above the cap rail. Use the thinnest sliver of wood or a piece of pre-stiffened cordage to simulate the spreader bar above the simulated dead eyes. I have tried on several occasions to simulate the "ratlines" (rope ladders going to the mast tops as cross ropes to the shrouds) by gluing the finest of sewing thread. I was never pleased with the results and the glue stiffened the shroud which hindered the final collapse of the model. If you're modeling in a two-liter or larger bottle, hence a larger-scaled ship, this bit of detail might not be a problem.

At this stage the standing and running rigging are complete. Run through all the boom and gaff strings, pass them through the appropriate holes and through the trestle holes. **I do NOT pass these strings through the bowsprit.** They will be cut off at the mast point after insertion. See the plans and diagrams of *Victorine* in chapter 6 for more details of this.

The spars are next. A simple clove hitch can be glued from the rear of the mast. In this case the spar can have the freedom of rotation. If the spar is near any run through holes mount it directly below this opening not above. The sails when they are attached will make this a mechanical impossibility. All spars must have the ability to be "cock billed" to allow the freedom of rotation needed for insertion. I suggest applying the glue at the back end only.

Now for the running rigging. **All lines must run high to low while running fore and aft.** I cannot stress this point enough. Its a simple but undeniable physical principle. The ship cannot collapse fully as the opposite direction will call for expanded strings not loose ones. All of the rigging diagrams call for it this way. If you feel that some look better the other way, by all means make them as run through cordage and not stationary. On all the square rigged vessels I've combined the lifts and the braces, in this way one knot serves two purposes. Using natural or off-white thread, run the lifts around the spar above the knot and around the spar. (see diagram). Keep checking for impeded rotation before gluing the knots. Before running the braces decide on the spar position. Is your vessel running before the wind? Is she tacking? Are they wearing ship? Set the braces according to your sailing plan.

This next part is as much a matter of taste as it is technique. Are you going to model sails at all? Will the ship exhibit a full suit, or will some be furled? Each diagram gives a full sail plan. The decision rests with you.

For sails I use a good grade of bond or linen paper in an off-white tone. The lighter the weight the better. If pure white is the only one available to you then try staining it with a weak tea solution. Some papers "pill" when dampened, so test a piece before deciding. Make a rough cut of the sail against your model, and not the plan. A small discrepancy, even as little as 1/16 of an inch from my plans to

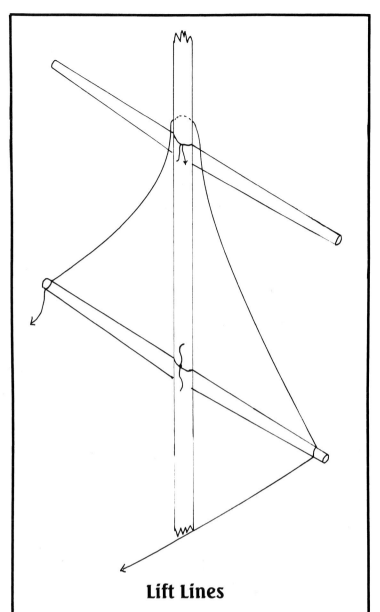

Lift Lines

These extra running lines are most impressive rigged as they are behind the sails. It is most important that they run free above the clove hitch that holds the spar in place. Otherwise the yard will not cock bill (rotate), making insertion an impossibility. Apply glue only at the spar ends.

your model, will make a difference. I use the fine pencil for the seam lines and a fine marker for the "reef points". These were ropes attached to the sails to shorten them in strong winds or gales. "Bunt lines," on the other hand, were used to haul sails in. Again, these can be simulated with pencil or marker. Seams should be the same on both sides. Use a white glue in sail making and mounting. The acetate type will stain, and the CA will change both the texture and transparency of the paper. To simulate furled sails, very fine tissue wrapping paper can be rolled up and attached to the spar. Bond paper is too thick to roll. Bunts can be tied around them. Roll each completed sail around a pencil

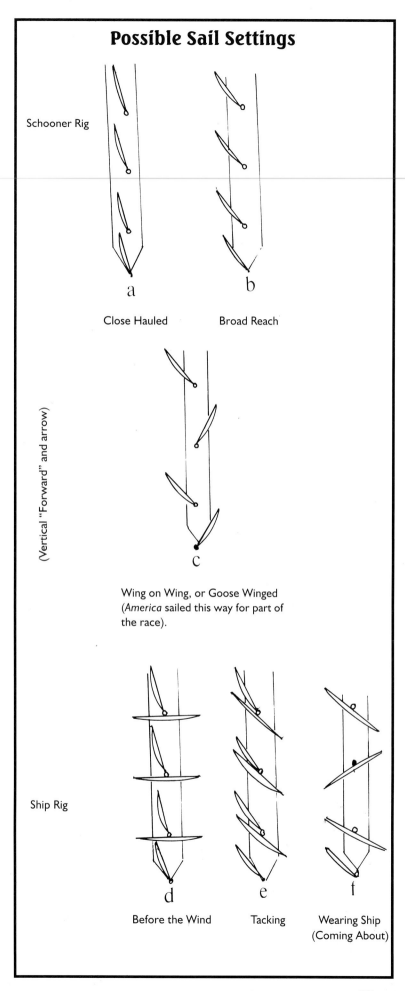

Possible Sail Settings

Schooner Rig

a
Close Hauled

b
Broad Reach

(Vertical "Forward" and arrow)

c

Wing on Wing, or Goose Winged
(*America* sailed this way for part of
the race).

Ship Rig

d
Before the Wind

e
Tacking

f
Wearing Ship
(Coming About)

or dowel to simulate the effect of the wind. Exaggerate this, since the sails will straighten somewhat when the masts are collapsed for insertion. The jib sails are doubled to move freely up and down on the braces, as these lines are in reality erecting lines. The only exception are the ones mounted on the fore stay since this cord goes through the bowsprit. Roll these on a pencil after mounting.

After all the sails are mounted, test-collapse, making sure all the spars cock bill fully. The boom and gaff sails are pulled free of the model since these are inserted before the hull. Develop an erecting plan as to which strings to pull first. Its a good idea to number the cords with masking tape on the ends to set the sequence for you. As you begin to raise the masts and sails, there might be tangles. Practice freeing them with your lances, not your hands. The boom and gaff sail is the last one to be secured. Take your time. Applying too much pressure on the cords can snap a mast.

22

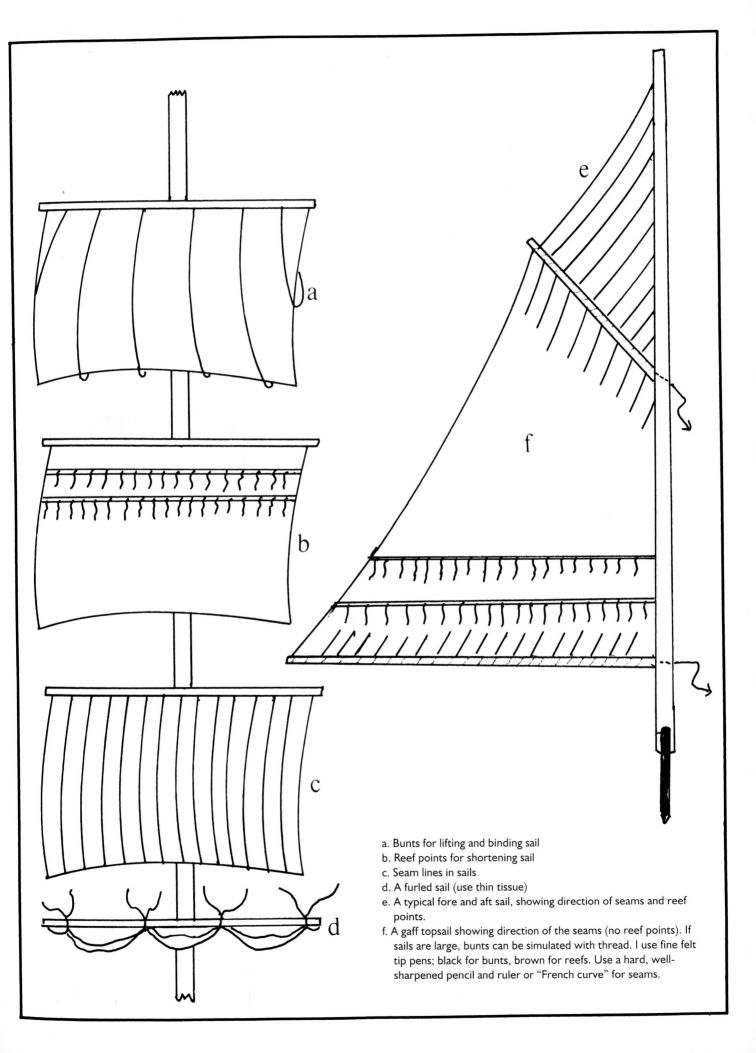

a. Bunts for lifting and binding sail
b. Reef points for shortening sail
c. Seam lines in sails
d. A furled sail (use thin tissue)
e. A typical fore and aft sail, showing direction of seams and reef points.
f. A gaff topsail showing direction of the seams (no reef points). If sails are large, bunts can be simulated with thread. I use fine felt tip pens; black for bunts, brown for reefs. Use a hard, well-sharpened pencil and ruler or "French curve" for seams.

Now comes the moment of truth. I would suggest that you read the next chapter before attempting to insert the model and raise the sails. As the Navy pilot was told upon coming in for a carrier landing with no fuel left in the tank, "you only have one shot at the deck!"

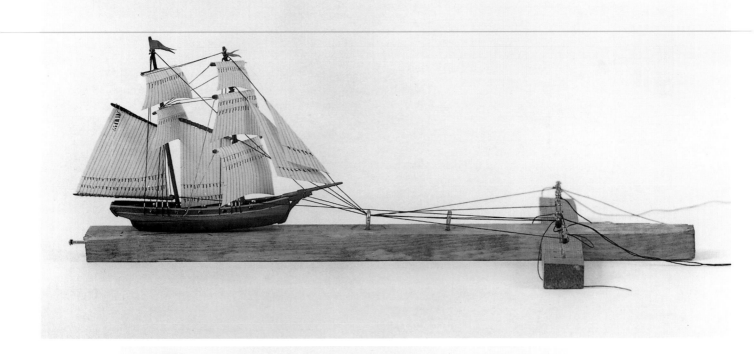

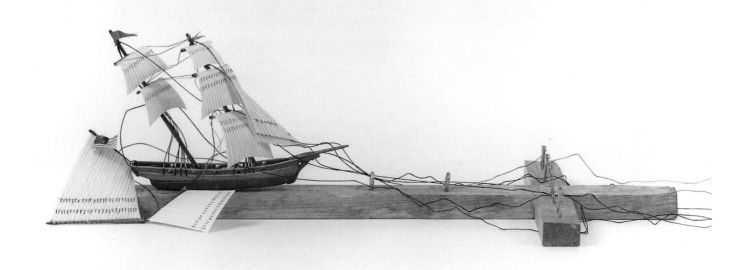

The Baltimore Privateer was fully rigged to sail before the wind on a slight starboard track. In the first stages of collapse, the fore and aft sails on the fore and main masts are pulled free and set back before the masts are fully dropped.

Chapter Five
Insertion and Erection

Tis not complete 'til it's sealed

To the person who once said, "One picture is worth a thousand words" this chapter is seventeen thousand words long. The following sequence is for the Hudson River sloop *Victorine* going into a one-liter scotch bottle. The clay sea has already been prepared and scooped to receive the hull. All the tools were in easy reach. I fashioned a lance with a small loop of wire 1/16 inch in diameter to hold a drop of CA glue. Because of the capillary action a drop will remain in the wire "eye" until it touches the bowsprit and strings. The glue will run off when contact is made.

Work slowly with good lighting. If you're prone to "salty language" you might get plenty of practice as the process unfolds. Good luck, and remember, those Ancient Mariners were able to do this on a rolling and pitching deck, with fewer tools and less lighting then you.

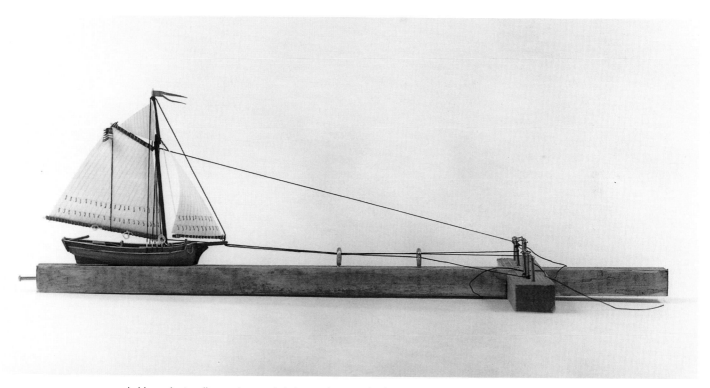

1. Here she is, all complete and sitting on her trestle. It seems a waste to remove her. However, the purpose of this book is bottling ships, not building stationary models. Did you forget anything? Deadeye paint? Strakes? Anchors? Are the sails secure? Now's the time to correct any minor flaws.

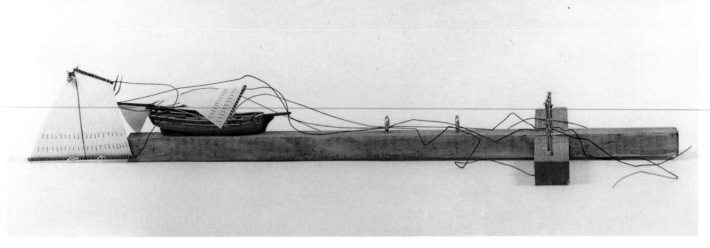

2. Collapse her carefully by first releasing all the boom and gaff strings. Cock-bill the yards, and roll up those jibs. Now, remove her from the trestle!

3. Is the sea to your liking? Have you prepared an indentation for the hull? Are all the whitecaps in place? Are all of the tools within easy reach? If you are using the plasticene clay for the "water" then this is most important. Cut a piece of paper to fit over the water in the bottle. That clay has a tendency of staining the sails blue. This paper bed will be removed *after* the masts are erect and boom and gaffs snug. Along the same line of thinking, make sure the neck of the bottle is spotless.

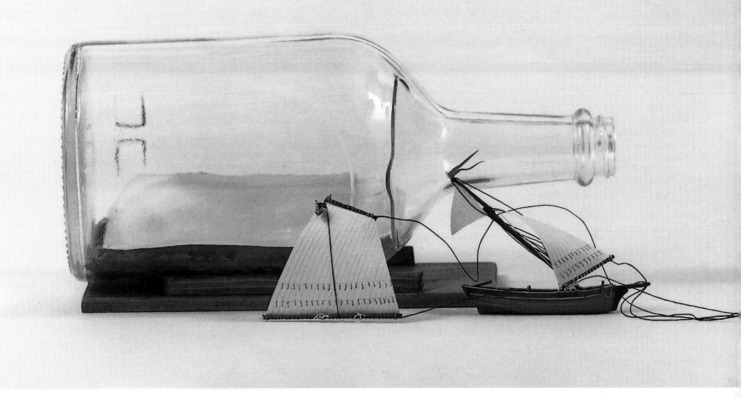

4. Measure the collapsed ship against the bottle. Try to envision the way the boom and gaff will lay inside. If the bed appears to be too far back or forward, adjust now.

5. Insert the boom and the gaff sails first. Coil in the direction of the billow. Slide it deep enough to avoid the folded masts.

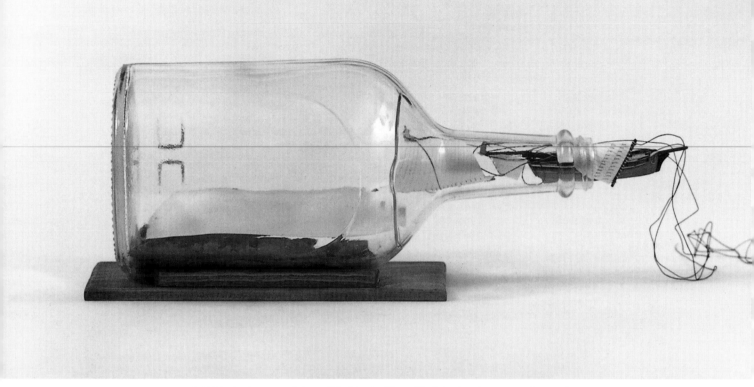

6. With the boom and the gaff inside the "barrel" of the bottle, start to insert the ship. Be careful with the sails, lest you crease them. The jib, with its attached club, has to be worked with care. I wrapped the sail around the hull.

7. She's in all the way!

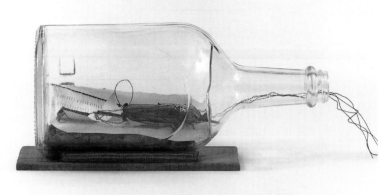

8. Laying on the paper bed (I told you this was necessary), she looks like a tangled lump. Remember, the hardest part is over. You got it in! All of those measurements actually worked out.

9. Grab the bow with a pair of long tweezers and slowly raise the mast. It doesn't have to be snug now, just up. You are first trying to get those sails out of the water.

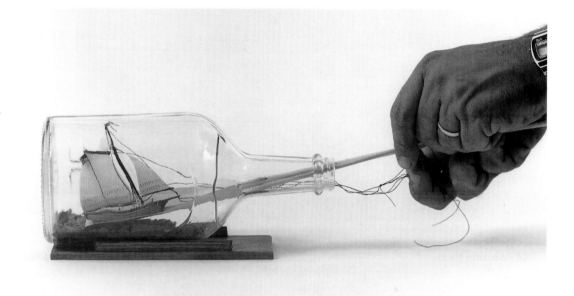

10. Pull the boom and the gaff strings in sequence, first one and then the other until snug against the mast.

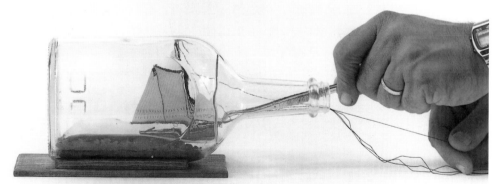

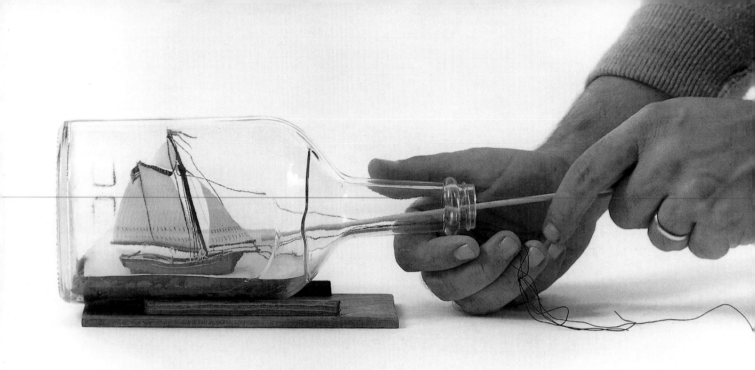

11. Reposition the hull and begin to snug up the mast.

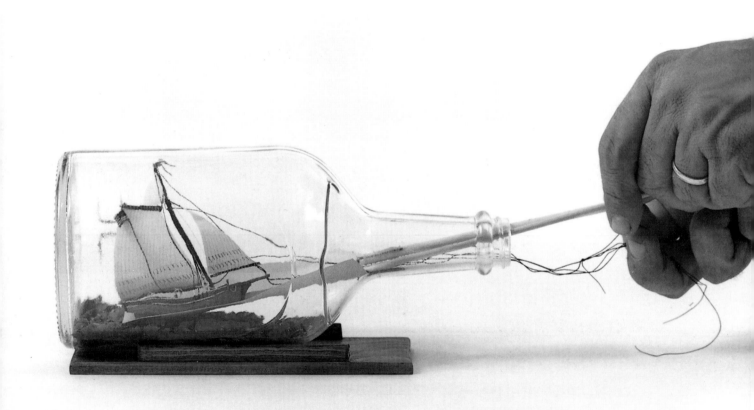

12. Holding the ship back with one of the lances, remove the paper bed. It should curl and come back out of the neck easily. Be cautious so as not to snag strings.

13. Using the bent lance, a knitting needle, or one of the coat hanger tools, "plant" the hull. Make sure that your tools are free of clay. A blob of clay on the outside neck will secure the strings.

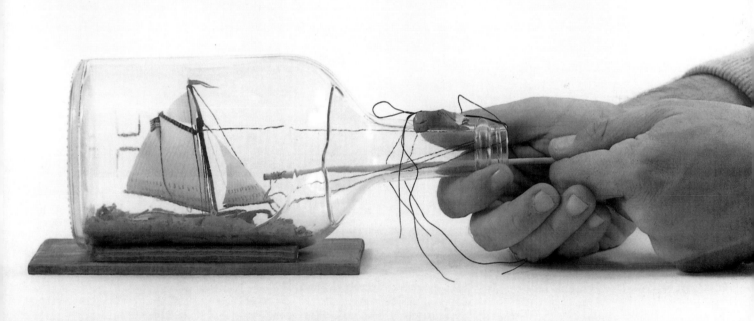

14. At this point, apply crazy glue to the erecting and boom and gaff joints. The tool mentioned in the opening paragraph is excellent, but a thin stick will do. Try not to get glue on the sails or sides of the bottle.

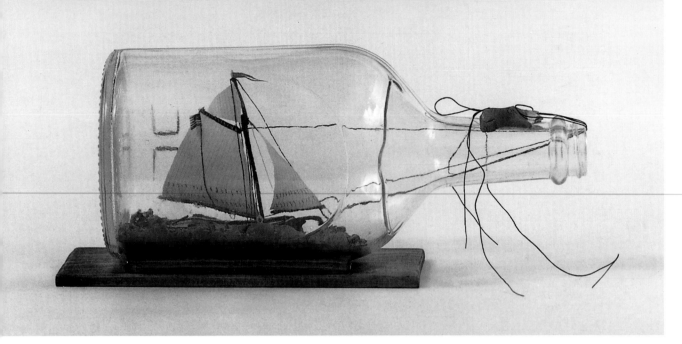

15. Let that glue dry!

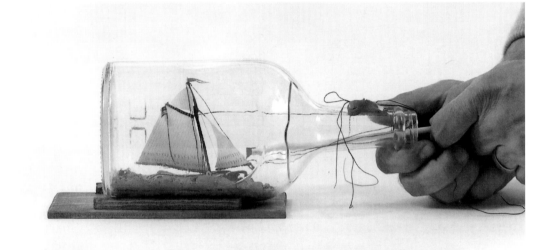

16. Try to make the cuts as clean and close as possible. See if the fabricated cutters reach the points easily. If not, refabricate.

17. Finished at last. All we need is a cork, a fancier stand, and a stiff drink. That's one way of getting more bottles.

All sails set and running before the wind, *America* shows her flags proudly.

America

America sailed low, cutting the water rather than plowing through it.

Being set at a slight starboard tack, the *Forester* fills the entire barrel of the bottle that houses her.

Forester

**Baltimore Clipper
(Italian Livery)**

Baltimore Clipper Privateer *Guerriero*, with a small model of the *Victorine* in the foreground. Ships in relative scale.

The port and starboard views clearly show the standing and running rigging against the sails. Note the boom and gaff strings being pulled away from the hull.

Baltimore Clipper

Baltimore Clipper
(Italian Livery)

The ship fills the bottle, with mast tips barely missing the top of the bottle.

Builder's-eye view of completed model.

36

This version of the *Victorine* is built only of natural wood. Cherry hull, basswood strake and caprail, walnut bullwarks and mast. The only paint used is on the mast and boom tips, and the deadeyes.

Here is the little *Victorine*, all sails set on a port tack in choppy seas. Note the anchor cable through the hawse hole, and tie line coiled in the shrouds.

I decided to mount this *Victorine* a little differently. The bottle is still the one-liter variety. Note the railing on the quarter deck.

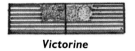

Victorine

38

I built this kit several years before as part of an HO scale diorama. Recently, I decided to take the measurements off the model and build her again in a bottle. It was bottled in four pieces.

Here is an example of a bottle in need of a ship. The "clay" sea is set and a permanent stand has been built.

The sloop *Victorine* in bottles of different sizes and shapes.

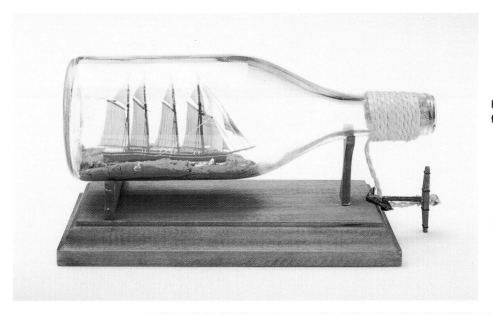

Here is the completed *Forester,*
forever sailing on a placid ocean

A model of the
Baltimore built clipper
with guns run out
sailing full before the
wind.

The rigging trestle with several hulls showing the beginning rigging detail. (Chapter 2)

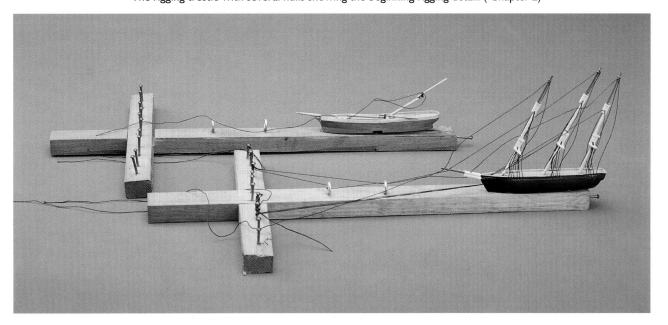

Inside this four-ounce bottle with a small neck is a fishing dory complete with sail, two fishermen and a line in the water.

Chapter Six
Hudson River Sloop *Victorine,* circa 1850
Commerce of the time, lifeblood of a nation

The inland waterways of colonial America were her commercial lifeblood before roads and railways were built. The Hudson River was no exception. The Port of New York with its myriad of wharves and shipyards was a major port of entry for most of the commerce of the north. These little sloops with their shallow draft and easy rig were the small carriers to and from the main port. Because of them, Albany and Syracuse were able to take advantage of the fortunes of trade. In fact, the New York Central Railroad was to lay its tracks along the Hudson River, taking advantage of the port towns as its stations. It was referred to as the "Water Level Route". Some of these sloops and those with similar rig were used across Long Island Sound linking Connecticut, Massachusetts, and Rhode Island to the main port.

I have chosen the little *Victorine* as the first model since it has such a simple rig and sail plan. I designed it to use only one string for mast erection and only three others to set the sails and trim.

The plans show complete rigging and sails, and with a little bit of patience, this model can be fully detailed. I built this model four different ways in two different bottle shapes. She is pictured several times in various chapters. You will see her in color, natural oak, walnut and boxwood. Whichever hull you choose the steps are identical, even for the vertical mounting.

The measurements on the plan will fit any bottle with a 3/4-inch neck and a minimum of 3 3/4-inch inside height. As mentioned before, measure the bottle first. You can "bootleg" about 1/4 to 1/2 inch off the mast if it suits the bottle. Anything more and the ship will appear too squat for its hull size. The main hull block is 2 1/2 x 5/8 x 3/8 inches. Measure the dead rise and deck shape directly from the plan. Take your time in carving, wood filler is of no use if you want a natural finish.

Next, lay the deck planking, clamping firmly with clamps or rubber bands until dry. Finish the hull carving as though the planking strip were part of it. Doubling up a piece of planking is sufficient for the quarter-deck. After planking I stained the deck to accentuate the plank lines. I used a thin brown acrylic rubbed in to fill the plank lines, sanding after drying, but almost any of the stains will do. This gave me a warm brown finish to the deck with dark brown lines. Use 1/16 square stock for the bulwarks, soaking first and notch-

Detail Sheet 1
Not to scale

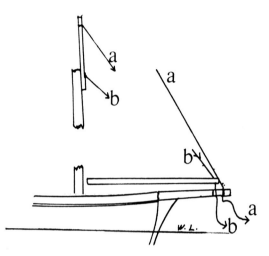

The mast stay (a) must run in front of the jibstay (b). If made to run through two separate holes, the bowsprit might weaken. I used and recommend a single, somewhat elongated hole. The jibstay (b) should run through the "club" (boom) at the foot of the jibsail.

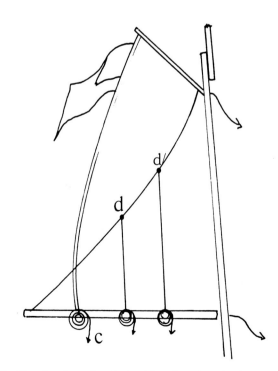

The "lazy boy" running rigging (d) ends with coils of rope attached to the boom. Put a drop of glue at the knots (d) and trim close. A small drop of brown paint will simulate blocks here.

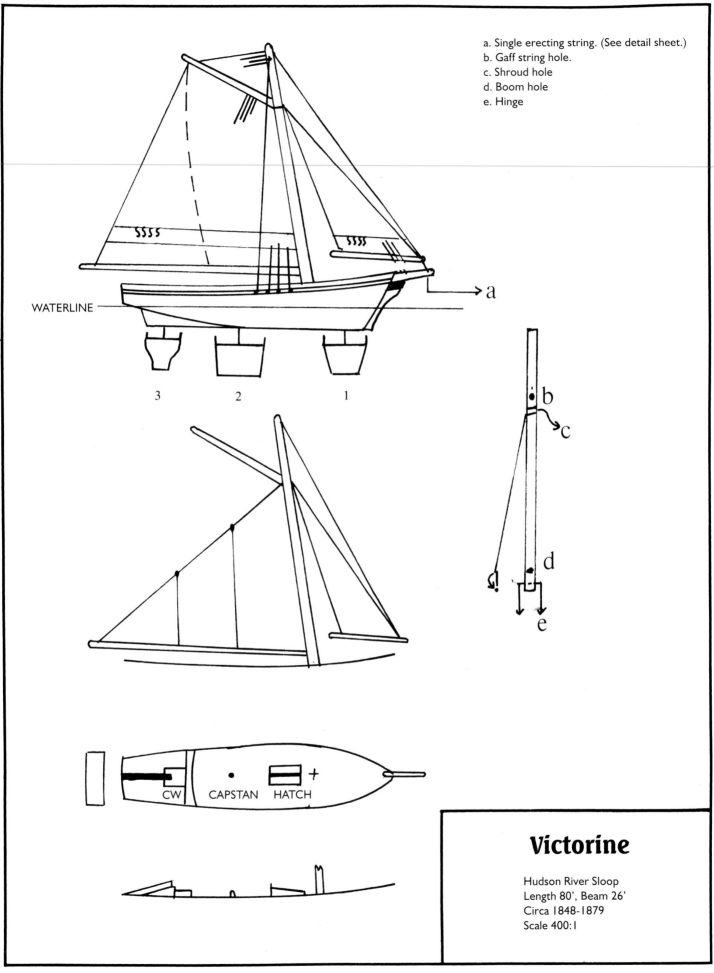

a. Single erecting string. (See detail sheet.)
b. Gaff string hole.
c. Shroud hole
d. Boom hole
e. Hinge

WATERLINE

3   2   1

a

b

c

d

e

CW   CAPSTAN   HATCH   +

Victorine

Hudson River Sloop
Length 80', Beam 26'
Circa 1848-1879
Scale 400:1

ing for the bow. The cut water is fitted to the bow with a liberal application of CA. After this feature dries it can be sanded and shaped.

Color scheme

Hull	Dark brown, black or natural
Masts	Natural or walnut
Starches	White, light gray, or natural
Deck furniture	Tan, white or walnut
Anchor	Black, with brown stock
Standing rigging	Black or dark brown
Running rigging	white, tan, or gray
Capstan	Black or brass
Cap rail	White, tan, or natural
Rub rails	White tan, or natural

After the hull is painted, attach it to the trestle. At this time add the transom and cap rails. I used 1/32 x 1/4 for the transom and 1/16 x 1/64 for the cap rails. If these sizes are not available, try to sand down the thinnest that's available. A credible cap rail can be made from strips of brown craft paper. Be careful, you want this feature to enhance the ships' appearance, not make it appear bulky. White or tan thread stiffened with CA was used for the strakes. All deck furniture, capstan (pinhead with a paper wrap), and anchor can be added now. Shape and erect the mast after all the appropriate holes are drilled. You will notice on the *Victorine* used for the erecting sequence in the previous chapter I used a two-piece, or "made" mast. These sloops

Starboard view of the *Victorine* from the plans, sailing close-hauled to the starboard.

were built both ways. I suggest that you use the two-piece version since you can drill a bigger hole for the stays without sacrificing structural strength. If you have chosen this as your first experience, perhaps this point of possible disaster can be avoided. Drill four holes through the bulwarks at deck level **behind** the mast line for the stays. Allow 1/16 between each hole. If the bulwark appears to be too thin it can be reinforced with CA before drilling.

I have found it easier to completely rig a model before adding sails, but that is a matter of choice. The boom and gaff should run free through their rigging holes as well as

The *Victorine* with a painted hull sailing on a broad reach. Mast height was slightly modified for the bottle.

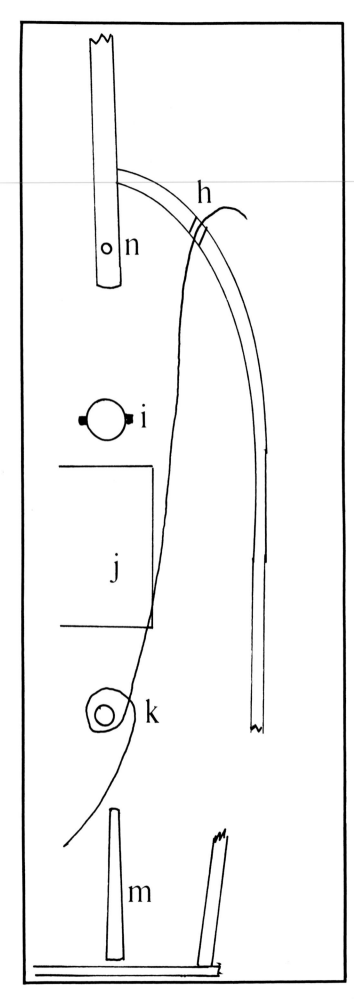

the erecting string(s). At this time you should be test collapsing the model and checking for possible snags. Add the sails and keep on testing.

As a rule of thumb (who is this thumb person?), I wait at least a day before bottling a model. I want to begin that odyssey with a fresh set of nerves. The photo sequence of my little *Victorine* entering her permanent berth is self-explanatory.

This successful venture should more then whet your appetite for the challenges of this hobby. This writer advises that you tackle each project slowly, and try not to make a full-rigged clipper ship with all sails set your second choice.

Congratulations, you are now in possession of a piece of history, first as an art form, and second, as the ship it represents.

Victorine
Not to scale

h. Hawse hole through bullwark (starboard only).
i. Position of mast (relative).
j. Forward hatch.
k. Capstan (small belaying pin or thick pinhead). Anchor rope coiled about with free end aft.
m. Tiller (small piece of wood pr pre-glued thread).

Chapter Seven
Schooner Yacht *America,* circa 1851

The Cup, the glory, and the legend

The yacht *America* evokes a lore of the sea that continues to this day in the famous race. She is an excellent choice for our second offering with a fairly simple rig and two masts. The *America* was afloat well into our century with a famous and varied career. First, and foremost, this was the yacht for which the "Americas Cup" race is associated, the pride of the yachting world. It seemed that the trophy was permanently housed and honored by the New York Yacht Club, but as you can recall or research, you know that this is changed.

The yacht itself was built in the early spring of 1851 for one specific purpose; to enter the English challenge race that year. What a ship! Her severe hull lines went steps farther then the Baltimore Clippers she was designed after. Some say it was her expert handling that brought her to ultimate victory, but in fact when she crossed the Atlantic on her maiden voyage, both ship and crew were untried. Others congratulate her sail makers for using close woven American linen, as opposed to the coarser English fabrics, in the ship's ability to "capture the wind". whatever the reasons, crew, sails, or the ship itself, she challenged and beat the best that the British had to offer at the time, sending home Queen Victoria's trophy still called the "Americas Cup" in her honor.

There are stories and legends about this race. first her master decided to add an extra sail before the start of the

Port and starboard view of *America* as she appeared at the start of her historic race. All sails are set including the last-minute flying jib. She is on starboard tack and her flags are set accordingly.

Port and starboard view of *America* as she appeared at the start of her historic race. All sails are set including the last-minute flying jib. She is on starboard tack and her flags are set accordingly.

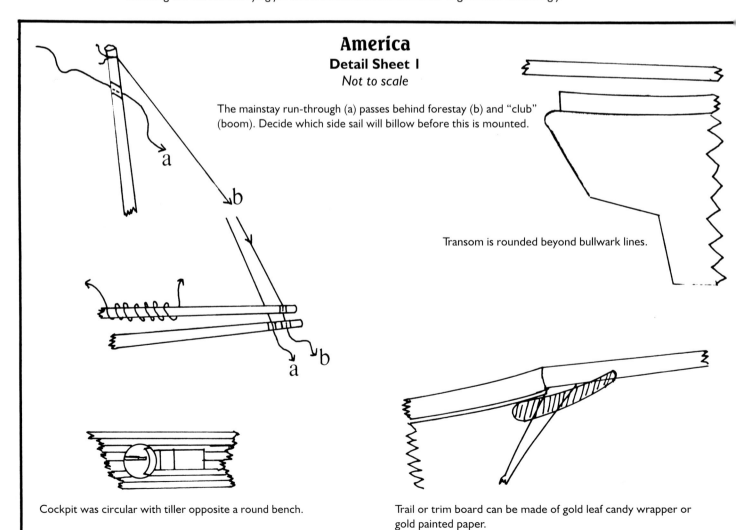

America
Detail Sheet 1
Not to scale

The mainstay run-through (a) passes behind forestay (b) and "club" (boom). Decide which side sail will billow before this is mounted.

Transom is rounded beyond bullwark lines.

Cockpit was circular with tiller opposite a round bench.

Trail or trim board can be made of gold leaf candy wrapper or gold painted paper.

race. It was a flying jib attached to a spar that elongated her bowsprit. It actually hampered her sailing qualities, and when carried away by the wind in mid-race, her sailing qualities improved. As the story goes, Queen Victoria, an avid yacht enthusiast herself, watched from a vantage point on shore. She asked after *America* crossed the finish line, who was second. The quote, dressed up by folklore and the press of the time was; "*America* is first, there is no second!"

After the race, when all the fanfare died down, she was sold to a wealthy Englishman and was used as a pleasure and racing craft throughout Europe for the next ten years. Next, she entered the American civil war as a blockade runner for the South, a very interesting fact in her career. The English were not the least bit thrilled of the Union blockade of Southern ports so they outfitted several "runners" to bring contraband in. The *Camille* (a.k.a. *America*) made several trips in this trade, and then went missing for more than a year. She was found quite by accident scuttled on the James River. The Union Navy refloated and refitted her, commissioning her into the navy as a Cutter and blockade vessel. They armed her with two deck guns and a swivel cannon. They added a square sail on the foremast and several flying jibs. She performed well in this incarnation and finished the war as a training ship for midshipmen at the Naval Academy in exile at Newport, RI. She became a private yacht again after the war and participated in several races in the 1870s and 80s, giving a good account of herself on more than one occasion. Through some complicated financial dealings, she was sold back to the Navy in 1891 for the sum of one dollar. At that time there were moneys donated by private citizens for her complete refit and overhaul; however, due to laws of the time, the Navy could not accept these funds and she remained rotting at Annapolis as a curiosity until 1939. Then, she was hauled out of the water to be refitted and a shed was constructed around her to prevent further damage. Because of wartime demands on shipyards in general, the refit was never finished. In March of 1942 a freak snowstorm hit the Maryland area. The shed collapsed under the weight of the snow, destroying her. Today, all that remains are several of her artifacts, displayed at the Naval museum at Annapolis and several others throughout the country. The cup is still vital to yacht racing, so her legacy lives on.

Four different deck and sail plans from the various stages of her career are included here. The model as executed depicts her at the start of the race at Cowes in 1851 with the flying jib in place. Construction is identical for all the sail and deck plans.

America
Detail Sheet 2—Alternative Sail Plans
Not to Scale

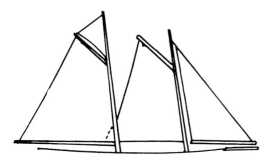

Her original sail plan; the way she appeared at the end of the Race in 1851.

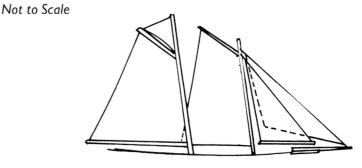

Original sail plan, with a flying jib added to a spar attached to bowsprit. This was her suit at the start of the Race in 1851.

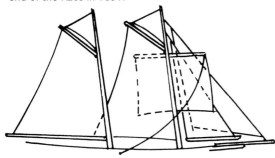

Civil War cutter rig. This is the *America* as a blockade vessel for the Union. In addition, she carried three cannon.

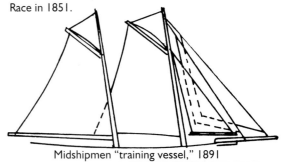

Midshipmen "training vessel," 1891

America
Two-masted racing yacht
Built: Wm. H. Brown Shipyard, New York, 1851
Designed: George Steers
Scale: 750:1

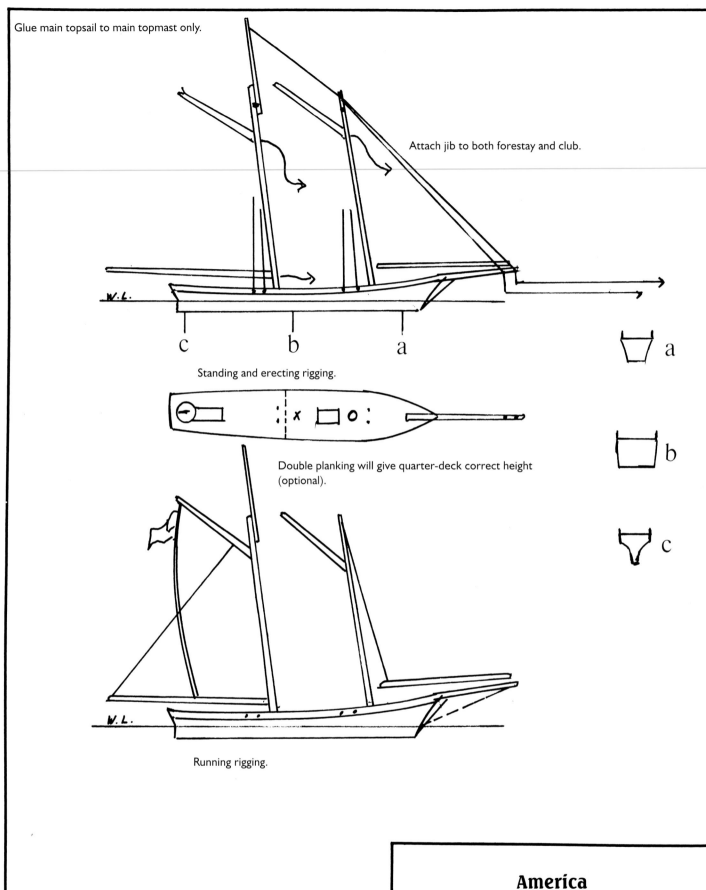

Glue main topsail to main topmast only.

Attach jib to both forestay and club.

W.L.

c   b   a

a

Standing and erecting rigging.

b

Double planking will give quarter-deck correct height (optional).

c

W.L.

Running rigging.

America

Scale plan for masts, booms, hull, and rigging.
Scale 750:1

Use a clear piece of basswood for the hull, carving and sanding the dead rise according to the plans. The deck planking is doubled to give the quarter-deck the necessary height. The curve of the transom is best molded in three pieces of the wood used for the bulwarks and finished with sandpaper to get the flowing curve. When adding the masts allow for the severe rake of the prototype; this will add to the illusion of speed.

The masts themselves are measured directly from the plan. The mainmast is doubled at the top and is much higher than the foremast. However if you're rigging her as a Civil War-era cutter, then double the foremast and add the square sail.

As simple as the *Victorine* was, *America* has a bit more deck detail. Her rounded cockpit was distinctive along with her low cabin.

Using several coats of sanding sealer on the hull, be careful of the sanding, as the thin wood for the bulwarks leaves no margin for error.

After the masts are inserted, mount the hull to the rigging trestle. Make the several trial collapses as you add the deck details, fixing potential problem areas as they might arise.

The shrouds are rigged first, allowing for the severe rake of the masts. I added the wale or strake after the shrouds were in place to hide the holes in the bulwark. The fore stay has two functions, that of raising the mast itself, and supporting the foresail. (I used two on my model, one as described, and the other for the flying jib) The main-stay mounts just below the fore stay and can be made to run through the same hole. Be careful when running double lines through the same bowsprit hole.

Color Scheme

Hull	Black
Deck	Natural
Inside bulwark	Off-white
Strake	Natural or white
Cockpit and tiller	Dark brown
Masts, boom, and gaffs	Natural, walnut, or cherry
Capstan	Black
Cannons	Black or brass
Lifeboat	White

Follow the rigging and sail diagram of your choice, again testing and collapsing to check for snags. A brief historical note about the sails. *America* sailed with tight sails showing very little billow. This added to her efficiency in racing. However, at this scale a slight billow will give the illusion of some movement. This is at best a personal choice.

After the sails and rigging are set to your satisfaction, collapse the model and insert as per Chapter Five. With *America*, as with the other multimasted models you will try, it is best to raise the masts from the front first. This way the stays, boom and gaff lines will run smoother through their erecting points. I set my model on a slight heel to the starboard. In this position the deck details can be viewed from either side of the bottle. Now you have *America*, forever captured in your imagination and on the bottled sea she sails.

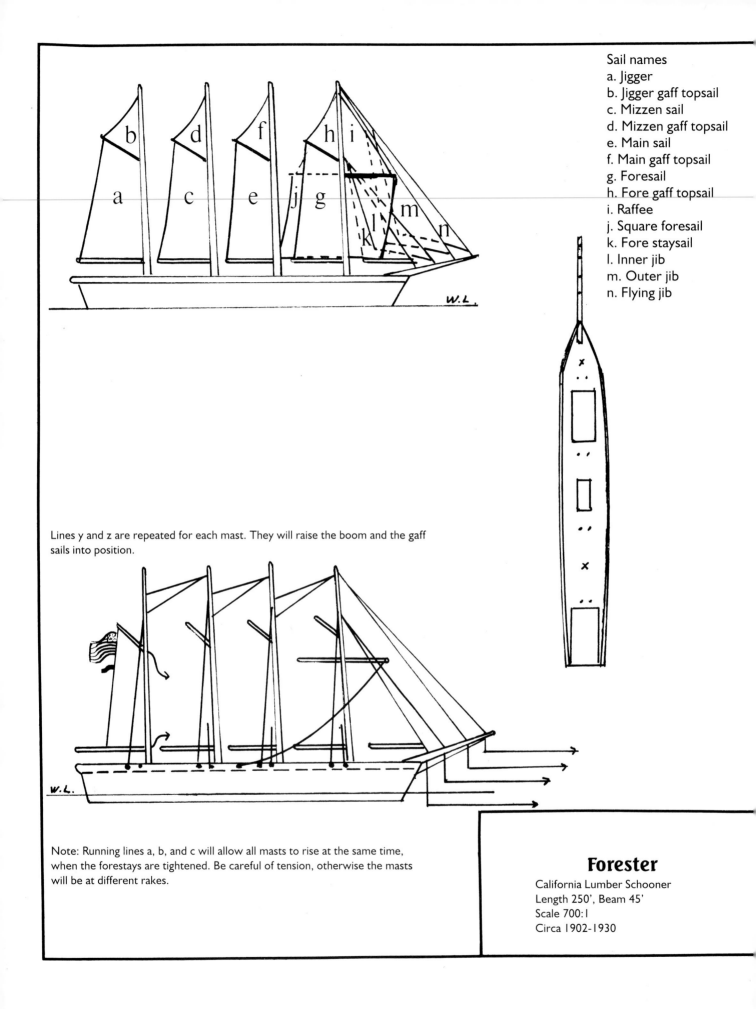

Sail names
a. Jigger
b. Jigger gaff topsail
c. Mizzen sail
d. Mizzen gaff topsail
e. Main sail
f. Main gaff topsail
g. Foresail
h. Fore gaff topsail
i. Raffee
j. Square foresail
k. Fore staysail
l. Inner jib
m. Outer jib
n. Flying jib

W.L.

Lines y and z are repeated for each mast. They will raise the boom and the gaff sails into position.

W.L.

Note: Running lines a, b, and c will allow all masts to rise at the same time, when the forestays are tightened. Be careful of tension, otherwise the masts will be at different rakes.

Forester

California Lumber Schooner
Length 250', Beam 45'
Scale 700:1
Circa 1902-1930

Chapter Eight
California Lumber Schooner *Forester*, circa 1900

Unsung hero, draught horse of the Pacific

The period in our history commonly referred to as the "Gay Nineties" saw much experimentation in deep water sailing vessel design. Fine steamships were built, all vying for the passenger and immigrant trade on both oceans. Warships were becoming obsolete quickly as new designs replaced them. Bulk cargoes, however, did not require speedy delivery or fancy arrival schedules. The nitrate boats of the South American trade and the American lumber boats are prime examples of this. They traveled routes with few coaling stations, and besides, coal would take up valuable cargo room. *Forester* came to sail in seas that saw the "windjammers" ply their trade around Cape Horn in this magnificent twilight of sail. Four- and five-masted ships were not an uncommon sight, and the few remaining "clippers" ended their days hauling bulk cargo as stumpmasted relics of their earlier glory.

American designers experimented with four-, five-, and six- masted vessels. There was even a seven-masted monster built. The designs were excellent both for their sailing qualities and the limited amount of men that were needed to crew them . Most carried small donkey engines on board to operate winches needed in handling sails. The *Forester* was one of these. She was built in 1900 to handle Redwood cargoes from the American northwest coastal log-

The *Forester* with all sails flying full is set on a starboard tack. Note the "raffees" above he fore square sail. She personifies a ship in a bottle.

Forester
Detail Sheet
Not to scale

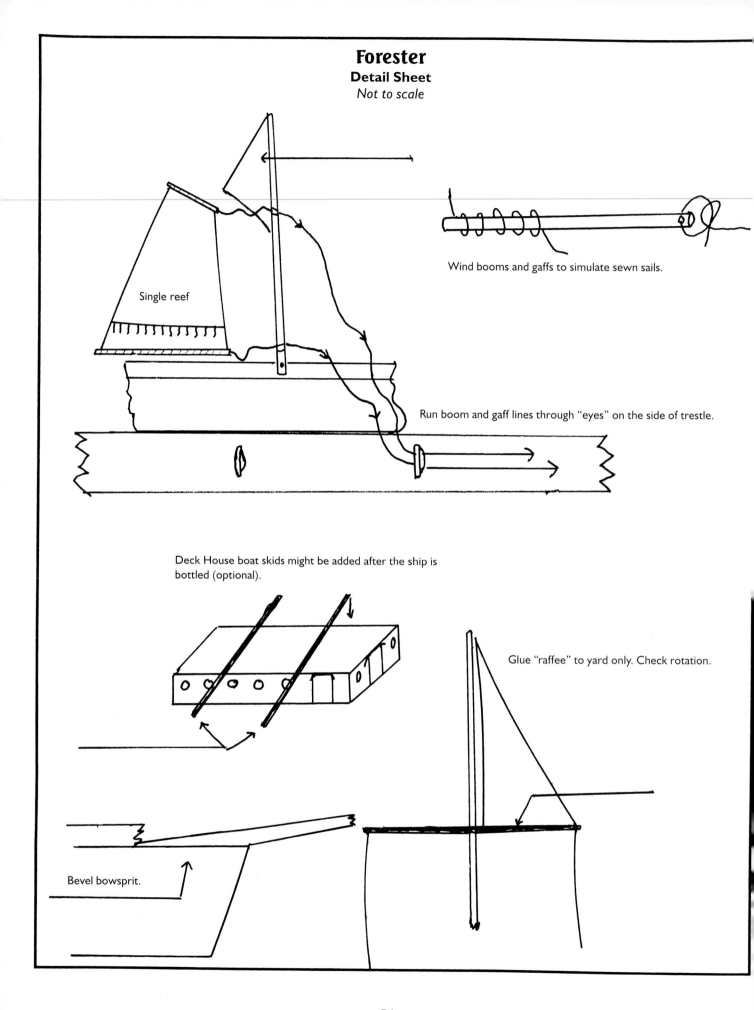

Wind booms and gaffs to simulate sewn sails.

Single reef

Run boom and gaff lines through "eyes" on the side of trestle.

Deck House boat skids might be added after the ship is bottled (optional).

Glue "raffee" to yard only. Check rotation.

Bevel bowsprit.

ging areas. All of her masts, boom, gaffs and sails were the same size, both for ease of handling and repair. She operated in this trade for twenty-two years, a tramp sailor at the end, defying the modern vessels that would eventually replace her. She lay beached on the Oregon coast from 1930 until she was destroyed by fire in 1975.

Here the *Forester* is modeled with all sails set, the interesting ones being the triangular ones on the foremast above the square foresail. These are called "Raffees". This was originally a Roman design in the days of its empire, and was proven useful again almost 2000 years later.

The hull design has no surprises to it. For the most part it is flush with very little dead rise. Add the bulwarks in the usual fashion, along with the fore and after deck houses. I fabricated the ship's wheel from a small watch gear.

As stated earlier, all masts, booms and gaffs are the same size. The biggest problem is to have all the masts at the same rake. I mounted a temporary stay across the tops of all the masts when the hull was fixed to the trestle, and did not remove this until all the shrouds were in place and secured. With the braces rigged as per the diagram, the entire upper hamper can be erected by pulling only on the fore stay. If you follow my design, only seven strings are necessary to set the mainsails, and one to set the jib.

Color Scheme

Hull	Black, white, or medium gray
Inside bulwarks	White or natural
Masts, boom, and gaffs	Natural or oak
Deck furniture	White
Sails	Tan or light gray

Modify the rigging trestle by adding two screw eyes on the side below the model to keep the rigging lines from tangling when building.

You might want to try a five- or six-masted version of this vessel since many of her sisters were built along the same lines.

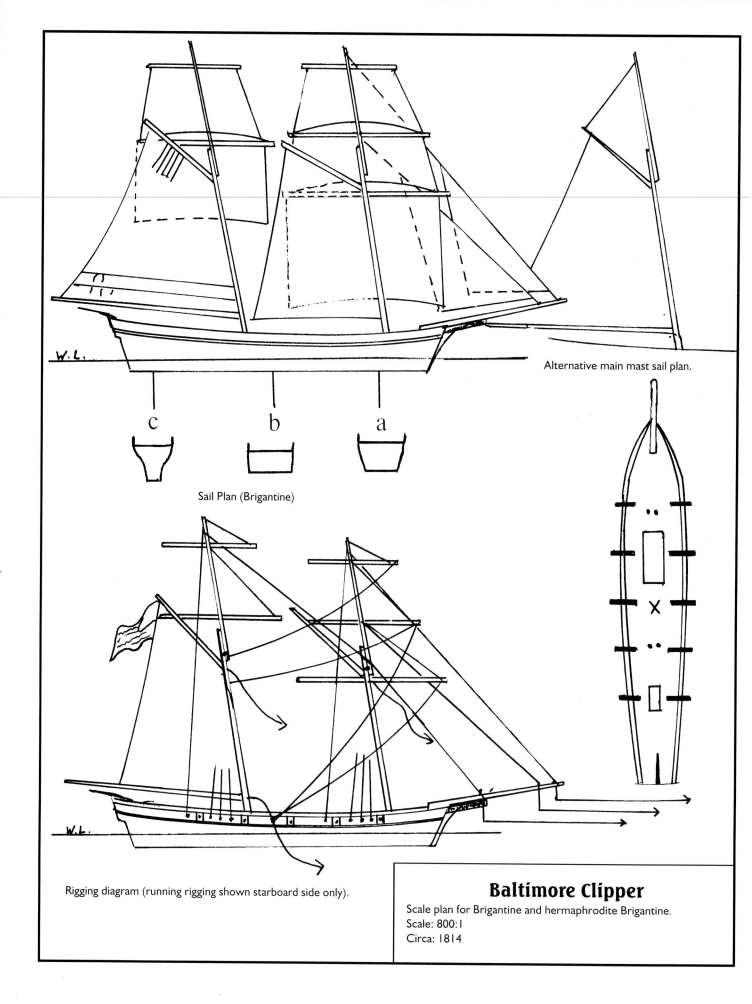

Alternative main mast sail plan.

c   b   a

Sail Plan (Brigantine)

W.L.

Rigging diagram (running rigging shown starboard side only).

Baltimore Clipper

Scale plan for Brigantine and hermaphrodite Brigantine.
Scale: 800:1
Circa: 1814

Chapter Nine
Baltimore Built Clipper Privateer, circa 1815

To sail free, against all flags

The terms "Baltimore Clipper" or "Baltimore Built" refer to a hull and sail configuration that is clearly an American design. The shape is an outgrowth of the Virginia-built pilot boats of the Revolutionary War period. The hulls were sharp with shallow drafts, and masts were set high with severe rake. The English used them as dispatch boats during the Napoleonic wars. Larger versions were used by America as privateers during our own English wars. Many were built, copied and modified during the first half of the eighteenth century. They ran the gamut of commerce of the time. With their swift lines and shallow draft, all the world's harbors were open to them. They were used by pirates, smugglers, slave traders, opium runners, as well as people with legitimate business needs. The ships sent to chase them, cutters by name, were usually built the same way. Their rig varied from full brig, brigantine, to hermaphrodite (foremast ship rigged, mainmast schooner rigged).

The model shown here was designed and built as a ten-gun privateer brigantine of the Napoleonic era. It was probably a ship like this that brought him back to France from Corsica. With her cherry wood hull, walnut bulwarks, basswood inlaid strakes and cap rail she is indeed a striking model. The natural wood sets off her brass cannons. I've included a generic color scheme as an alternative.

Begin with a 3 1/2 x 5/8 x 3/8-inch block for the hull. She is flush-decked but had a severe dead rise flowing aft from her foremast. Take your time with this detail.

Add the deck planking and bulwarks now. On the model as photographed, I laid the bulwarks over the bass deck planking; that's how I achieved the inlay effect of the strakes. With a basswood cap rail, the color scheme repeats. At this point add the bulwarks and transom first, but not the cap rail. Measure off and cut the gun ports now, unless you decide not to model with the guns run out. The cap rail can now reinforce the bulwark. I used 1/32 x 1/16-inch bass for this.

Color Scheme

Hull below bulwarks	Black or deep red
Bulwarks	Cream or buff
Cap rail	Natural or walnut
Masts, booms, and gaffs	Natural or walnut
Deck	Natural
Deck furniture	Natural
Strakes	Natural
Lifeboat	Buff or red
Cannons	Black or brass
Sails	Pale yellow, tan, or light orange
Mast tops	Black

If the rigging diagram is followed, the masts are raised with only three strings, and three will set the sails. However, this is the first model having multiple square sails and they require their own set of rules. The running rigging braces should run downward fore and aft. Unless this is followed, the model will not collapse fully. The yards must rotate fully lying parallel to the masts (lying a cockbilled was the term), otherwise she cannot be bottled. In real life ships did this when they were close-wharfed to each other.

Mount the cannons and masts at the same time as the bulwark/shroud clearances are important. Now mount the sails. If space allows, the lifeboat can be mounted before insertion. Otherwise a modified lance can be used. I set the square sails in a tack position based on the bottle I used.

The stays themselves, if set properly, will hold these sails in any position. Again, you can use the lances to tease them into position after bottling.

Port and starboard side views of my Privateer, in Italian livery. I've named her *Guerriero* ("warrior", in Italian). Her wood is cherry for the hull, basswood strakes, and walnut bullwarks. I designed her in order to get the most ship in a bottle this size.

Chapter Ten
Confederate Raider *C.S.S. Alabama*

True to a cause, gallantry and chivalry on the sea

The *Alabama* was afloat only two years for a Navy that lasted only four. The American Civil War conjures up many memories, most sad, horrible, and some romantic as it flows back into the corridors of time. The names that remain—Gettysburg, Shiloh, Antietam, the Wilderness, and the rest—are now tourist attractions to be visited and commemorated. But what of the Navies? There are no shrines or hallowed grounds to mark their passing. Only the sea remains, covering all that once was.

The *Alabama* was built for the Confederacy in Great Britain under the cloak and dagger politics of the period. England needed Southern cotton. She had already outfitted several blockade runners to try and keep the trade lines open, but the blockade was strengthening all the time. The *Alabama,* and her two sister ships, *Florida,* and *Shenandoah* were built for a different purpose. Their function was to sail the seas, destroying Yankee commerce wherever it was found. Trade ships, whaling ships, and sundry vessels were their targets. The plan was to free Southern ports of the blockade ships by forcing the overtaxed Union Navy to chase them.

Alabama sailed from Liverpool in July of 1862 bearing papers that identified her as the British merchantman *Enrica.* She sailed to the Azores to take on arms and a confederate crew. For twenty-two months she sailed both oceans, always one step ahead of the pursuit, managing to capture and destroy 52 Yankee vessels, many of them high-stepping clippers and whaling ships. It was an ironic twist of fate that she sunk the *Alert,* made famous by Richard Henry Dana in his American classic *Two Years Before The Mast.* Her bunkers only carried coal for fifteen days of sailing, so much of the time while not in action she stayed under sail alone. Under full sail with steam she could average 14 knots, more than enough to chase, catch, and elude.

Almost all English and French ports were open to he to refit, refuel, and repair. In June of 1864 she was put into Cherbourg, where she hoped to receive a complete overhaul. Napoleon III was friendly to the Southern cause, since they were keeping the Union busy, giving France a chance to invade Mexico.

Alabama was caught in harbor by the newly built Union warship *Kearsarge.* She came out of harbor to

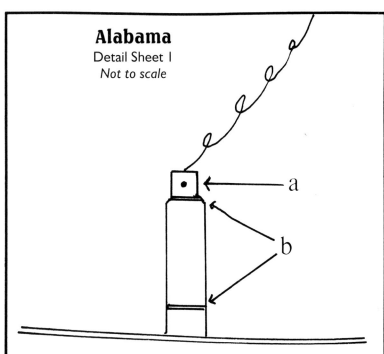

Alabama
Detail Sheet 1
Not to scale

Smokestack is fabricated from 1/8-inch dowel with small taper near the top.
a. Pinhole is drilled near the top and a bent lance is used to locate in position *after* ship is bottled.
b. Thin paper bands or pieces of pre-glued string.

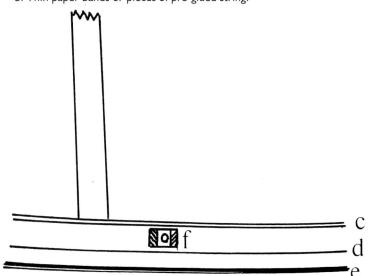

c. Cap rail
d. Upper strake, pre-glued string
e. Lower strake of thin wood
f. Gunport hatches. They opened to the side in two pieces. Fabricate out of paper. Painted the same color as inside the bullwark.

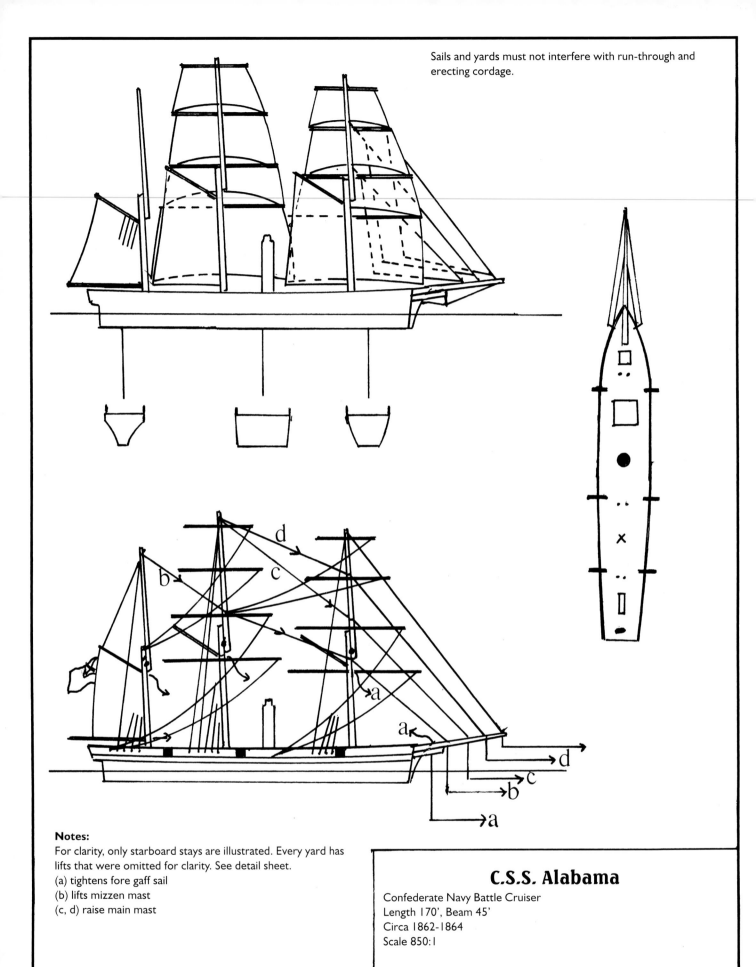

Sails and yards must not interfere with run-through and erecting cordage.

Notes:
For clarity, only starboard stays are illustrated. Every yard has lifts that were omitted for clarity. See detail sheet.
(a) tightens fore gaff sail
(b) lifts mizzen mast
(c, d) raise main mast

C.S.S. Alabama

Confederate Navy Battle Cruiser
Length 170', Beam 45'
Circa 1862-1864
Scale 850:1

Here she is in all her brief glory, all sails set, smoke pouring out of her funnels, guns run out, and sailing before the wind. She is set in with a high bow wave to give the illusion of speed and power.

fight for many reasons, least of which was the fear of being blockaded. Like two medieval knights, the ships jousted and parried, both being of almost equal speed and armament. The crew of the *Kearsarge* had shrouded her vital sides near the engine room with heavy anchor chain to ward off enemy fire. *Alabama* took several shots below the waterline, and began to slow down and sink. As she surrendered, most of her officers and crew were rescued by nearby English vessels that had come out to watch the fight, thereby avoiding capture. She sunk off the French coast, her short but defiant career over. In 1871 the English government paid 15.5 million dollars to the US for their part in building these raiders. This is historically known as the "Alabama claims."

The model was designed and planned as the she might have looked under full sail and steam. In keeping with this full American theme I planned her to fit a bottle of Jack Daniel's® Whiskey.

All measurements are taken with this in mind. Take your time on this one. The results with the smokestack are well worth it.

Begin with the hull, taking measurements directly from the plan. The Jack Daniels bottle has a flared neck with the smallest opening toward the front. Her hull should fit easily into this open space, only filling the lower semicircle. The gun ports on this model were opened with a drill and file after the cap rails were in place. The hatches for the ports are in two pieces and open to the side. I used painted sail paper for these. The masts and sails are rigged as the plan shows with no more surprises in the rig than the ship

in the previous chapter. *Alabama* was a three-masted bark and her erection should be smooth. Now that I've whetted your appetite, here is the hitch. The smokestack **cannot** fit through the bottle neck with the ship. I added this after the bottling. First, I drilled a hole to accept the stack through the deck planking into the hull. I built and test-fitted several times. Again, I modified one of my lances with a 90-degree bend and drilled a small but free-moving hole in the top of the stack to receive the lance pin. This will be covered by judicious teasing of the cotton "smoke". A little patience and the thing will go into place. With a drop of CA on the end of a lance and *Voila!* (there's that French word again) it's done.

Color Scheme

Hull	Black
Deck furniture and life boats	White
Masts	White to tops, natural or walnut uppers
Booms, gaffs, and spars	Natural or walnut
Cannons	Black or brass
Cap rail	Natural or walnut
Inside bulwarks	Buff or cream
Strakes	Upper white, lower natural or walnut

Someday I would like to model her again, in a larger bottle, trading punches with *Kearsarge*, but for now I am content to have her this way, a piece of American history in a distinctive American bottle.

Afterword

I tried in all cases to give you some of the historical background of these ships as well as all the hobby tricks I've learned. Needless to say you will discover many more on your own as you attempt to sail in glass bottles.

Thank you for sharing my hobby with me.

Fair winds, calm seas, and snug harbors.

Guy DeMarco August, 1999

Glossary of Nautical Terms and Expressions

There is not a "sea book" written that does not contain a short dictionary of specialized terms or expressions. With the advent of trivia games, this can be quite handy. You might even use some of these to spice up the narratives of your creations.

AFT- toward the stern, toward the back

ALOFT- Above the decks

AMIDSHIPS - At or near the center

ATHWART- At right angles to the fore and aft center line

BACK STAY- A shroud from the upper masthead leading down to the chain plates as a support for the mast. They were designed as a balancing force to overcome the pull of the sails.

BELAY- To make fast, to fasten, to stop.

BELAYING PIN- A wood or iron pin set in a socket to secure cordage.

BEND- To fasten in place, as in to "bend" a sail

BLOCK- A pulley

BINNACLE-Housing for the ships compass.

BOOM- The spar at the bottom of a fore and aft sail

BOW- Front of the ship

BOWSPRIT-The spar jutting out of the bow as a support for stays.

BRACES-Ropes to control yard position and swing

BULWARK- A closed or solid rail along a ships side.

CAPSTAN- An upright winch used to haul anchor or heavy lines

CUT-WATER-The forward timber of a ship (Stem)

COCKBILL- The ability of a yard to swivel on its mount to parallel the mast.

DEAD EYE- A round wooden block usually with three holes used to tighten shrouds and backstays

DEAD RISE- see SHEER

DOUBLING-The overlapping section of two mast timbers. The position usually referred to as a top, as in "fore-top".

DRAFT- The distance below the waterline

FAIRLEAD- A guide for a rope to change direction.

FIGUREHEAD- An ornament at the bow of a ship under the bowsprit

FORE-Toward or near the front.

FORECASTLE-The raised section of the deck at the bow. (pronounced "fo'cstle")

FOREMAST- On multimasted ships the one nearest the bow.

GAFF- A spar to stretch and hold the upper part of a fore and aft sail.

GUY- A line or purchase used to steady a boom.

HATCH- An opening in the deck.

JIB-A triangular sail set on a stay ahead of the foremast.

JIB-BOOM-A spar above the bowsprit. (The first words of an old Rock and Roll song)

KEEL-The bottom main timber of a ships construction

LEECH- The side edges of a square sail, and the after edge of a fore and aft sail

LUFF- The forward edge of a fore and aft sail

MAINMAST- Middle mast of a three masted vessel, second mast of a two masted one.

MAST HEAD- Top of a mast

MIZZEN MAST- Mast aft of the main mast

PEAK- The outboard end of a gaff.

PORT- The left side of a ship when facing forward.

QUARTER- The side of a vessel near the stern.

RAIL CAP-Flat covering piece on top of a rail or bulwark.

RAKE- The angle of a mast leaning aft.

RATLINES- The cross ropes on the shrouds to form ladders.

REEVE- To run a rope through a block or tackle.

RUNNING RIGGING- Ropes and blocks used to control sails and spars.

SALTY LANGUAGE- Terminology that is somewhat foreign sounding. Commonly used by coaches when speaking to losing teams at half time, people who bang their thumbs with hammers, drivers that close doors on their hands, and brave souls that try to bottle ships.

SHEER- The curve of the deck from bow to stern.

SHIP-Technically speaking a three or more masted vessel with square sails rigged on each mast. In general, any large vessel.

SHROUDS-Part of the standing rigging. Ropes from mast tops used to support masts.

SPANKER- The fore and aft sail on the last mast.

SPAR- Any boom, gaff, or yard.

STANDING RIGGING- All fixed rigging used to support masts, such as shrouds and stays.

STAY- A fixed rope to support a mast in the fore and aft position.

STEM- Forward timber of ship construction (See CUT WATER)

STERN- The back of a ship

STRAKE- A row of planking that forms that juts out from the hull. (Usually as a "rub rail") i.e. "Sheer Strake" is the row at the top of the hull below the bulwark.

TACK- To sail a vessel contrary to the wind.

TAFF RAIL - The railing about the stern of the vessel.

TILLER- A bar to control the rudder. On larger vessels the ships wheel controls the tiller with the aid of blocks and tackle.

TRANSOM- The flat upright part of a ships stern.

TUMBLE HOME - The inward slope of a ships side toward the bulwark.

WALE- An extra heavy strake on a ships side at the thickest part of the hull as a "rub rail" to avoid damage.

YARD- An athwart ship spar to set a square sail.

Appendix

I've included two excellent sources of supplies that have made this craft of mine easier. Catalogs are available from both.

Model Expo Inc.
PO Box 229140
3850 N 29 Terrace
Hollywood, FL 33022
Source of wood shapes, sizes and varieties. Paints, glue, specialized tools as well as miniature parts and nautical fittings that can be adapted to working in small scale.

Micro-Mark Inc
340 -2633 Snyder Ave
Berkeley Heights, NJ 07922-1595
A constantly growing and changing assortment of tools, parts, woods and paints, some of which are unique to this organization.

Footnote:
As we go into the next century the world wide web is changing the way we browse, buy and research. Search engines are constantly improving in both speed and accuracy with downloads that were beyond comprehension a few short years ago. To say that this is a valuable source is to belabor the obvious.